→ INTRODUCING

POLITICAL PHILOSOPHY

DAVE ROBINSON & JUDY GROVES

Published in the UK in 2011
by Icon Books Ltd.,
Omnibus Business Centre,
39-41 North Road, London N7 9DP
email: info@iconbooks.co.uk
www.introducingbooks.com

Sold in the UK, Europe, South Africa
and Asia by Faber and Faber Ltd.,
Bloomsbury House,
74-77 Great Russell Street,
London WC1B 3DA
or their agents

Distributed in the UK, Europe, South
Africa and Asia by TBS Ltd.,
TBS Distribution Centre,
Colchester Road, Frating Green,
Colchester CO7 7DW

This edition published in Australia
in 2011 by Allen & Unwin Pty. Ltd.,
PO Box 8500, 83 Alexander Street,
Crows Nest, NSW 2065

Previously published in the UK and
Australia in 2003

This edition published in the USA
in 2011 by Totem Books
Inquiries to: Icon Books Ltd.,
Omnibus Business Centre,
39-41 North Road,
London N7 9DP, UK

Distributed to the trade in the USA
by Consortium Book Sales & Distribution
The Keg House
34 Thirteenth Avenue NE, Suite 101
Minneapolis, Minnesota 55413-1007

Distributed in Canada by
Penguin Books Canada,
90 Eglinton Avenue East, Suite 700,
Toronto, Ontario M4P 2Y3

ISBN: 978-184831-203-6

Originating editor: Richard Appignanesi

Printed by Gutenberg Press, Malta

Questions

Political philosophers ask questions about individuals, communities, society, the law, political power, the State, and about how they all relate.

▶ Is it possible or desirable to say what human beings are "really like"?

▶ What is society? Is it something more than the people who live in it? Or was the British Prime Minister Mrs Thatcher right to say "There is no such thing as society"?

▶ What is the State? Is it an artificial construct or something that has naturally evolved?

▶ How free can the State allow individual citizens to be? Are there good moral reasons why citizens are obliged to obey the law? To what extent does the State have the right to punish those who disobey its commands?

▶ Is democracy the best form of government?

▶ Should the State be interested in furthering economic equality? If so, should it be allowed to interfere with other people's private property?

3

Back to Basics

Many political philosophers begin by concentrating on individuals. After all, societies and states are made up of individuals first, and governments must come after. Are political institutions simply the end result of attempts to fulfil the essential and universal needs of individuals? But what if we have no real knowledge about the needs and purposes of human beings? Besides, we aren't just dropped into society with all the ready-made capacities that make us human.

THERE CAN BE NO DOUBT THAT SOCIETY MAKES US.

EVEN OUR MOST "PRIVATE" THOUGHTS DERIVE FROM LINGUISTIC RESOURCES THAT AREN'T OUR OWN.

BUT EVEN THOUGH WE MIGHT ALL BE DERIVATIVE "SOCIAL PRODUCTS", NONE OF US FEEL WE'RE JUST ROBOTS.

PARADOXICALLY, WE ARE MADE BY SOMETHING THAT WE FEEL WE HAVE THE RIGHT (AND DUTY) TO QUESTION.

Natural Communities

The word "community" suggests something immediate, local and praiseworthy. Political philosophers think of communities as small groups of people with shared values who enjoy solidarity with little need of laws or hierarchical chains of command.

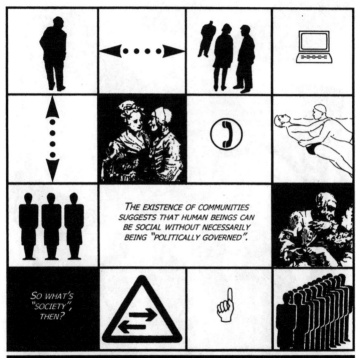

THE EXISTENCE OF COMMUNITIES SUGGESTS THAT HUMAN BEINGS CAN BE SOCIAL WITHOUT NECESSARILY BEING "POLITICALLY GOVERNED".

SO WHAT'S "SOCIETY", THEN?

SOCIETIES ARE LARGER THAN COMMUNITIES AND HELD TOGETHER BY COMPLEX SYSTEMS OF RULES, CUSTOMS AND INSTITUTIONS.

17th-century political philosophers made distinctions between free associations of individuals – **societies**, perhaps agreed on by some form of "contract" between individuals – and **States**, which are constituted by specific hierarchical power structures and the threat of coercion.

Society and State

Is it possible that we are all "social animals" but not necessarily political ones? Where is the evidence for non-political societies? Or is this an idealistic fantasy? Some philosophers believe that distinctions made between societies and States only lead to confusion. Societies can only exist if they are political. Power – and who **has** it – are features of human life that never go away.

THE "STATE" IS DEFINED AS AN AREA OF TERRITORY WITH AN ORGANIZED LEGAL SYSTEM AND A GOVERNMENT THAT HAS A "LEGITIMATE" MONOPOLY OF FORCE OVER ITS CITIZENS.

MODERN STATES HAVE ENORMOUS AND OFTEN **INTRUSIVE** AUTHORITY ...

THAT'S WHY PHILOSOPHERS ENDLESSLY REDEFINE WORDS LIKE "CONSENT", "AUTHORITY" AND "OBLIGATION".

What is Political Philosophy?

Most modern philosophers accept that moral and political propositions have no factual or logical status. Hence, it is impossible to prescribe what States should be or define what ought to be our relationship to them. Providing definitive answers to political problems must be ruled out.

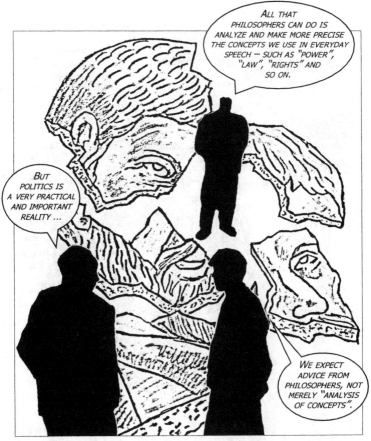

> ALL THAT PHILOSOPHERS CAN DO IS ANALYZE AND MAKE MORE PRECISE THE CONCEPTS WE USE IN EVERYDAY SPEECH — SUCH AS "POWER", "LAW", "RIGHTS" AND SO ON.

> BUT POLITICS IS A VERY PRACTICAL AND IMPORTANT REALITY ...

> WE EXPECT ADVICE FROM PHILOSOPHERS, NOT MERELY "ANALYSIS OF CONCEPTS".

But political philosophy is as ideological as any other kind of discourse. We accept from it what agrees with our normal core beliefs and values. This is why all political concepts are always "essentially contrasted".

Origins in Ancient Greece

The first people to write about political philosophy were the ancient Greeks.
To begin with they were "stateless" semi-nomadic tribes who finally settled
all over the coastal regions of the Aegean and Mediterranean.

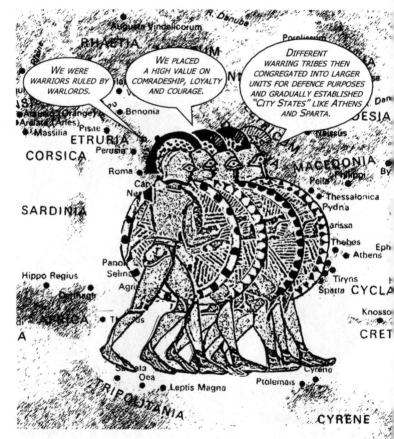

The "Polis" or City State was usually small and independent, and each one
was ruled by its own unique kind of government.

The City State of Athens

The most interesting and influential "Polis" was Athens, which experienced all sorts of governments. Political power had originally rested in the hands of a kind of aristocracy, similar to a tribal council, but gradually the citizen body itself acquired more and more power, and eventually ruled Athens between 461 and 322 BC.

The Duties of Citizens

Being an Athenian "citizen" was a serious business, involving duties as well as rights.

WE DO NOT SAY THAT A MAN WHO TAKES NO INTEREST IN POLITICS IS A MAN WHO MINDS HIS OWN BUSINESS; WE SAY THAT HE HAS NO BUSINESS HERE AT ALL.

THE POPULAR ASSEMBLY (I.E. THE "GOVERNMENT"), MADE UP OF ALL ADULT MALE CITIZENS, MET AT REGULAR INTERVALS TO DECIDE ON MATTERS OF STATE.

SO ATHENS WAS GOVERNED BY AMATEURS.

The population was small enough for this kind of "pure" democracy to work, and most Athenians seemed to have been immensely proud of their State. They identified with it so completely that it was virtually impossible for any of them to imagine a life outside it.

Direct Democracy

Athenians fought alongside each other in battle and were more "tribal" than we are now. Their social and political world was very different from ours. They had little conception of "the individual" as something separate from "the citizen" and only very hazy notions of private rights. Society and State were indistinguishable.

FOR MODERN PHILOSOPHERS AND HISTORIANS THIS IS A MAJOR HEADACHE.

MANY ANCIENT GREEK WORDS ARE ALMOST IMPOSSIBLE TO TRANSLATE, SO DEEPLY EMBEDDED ARE THEY IN THIS UNIQUE CULTURE.

THIS HASN'T STOPPED MOST OF US FROM HAVING FIRM OPINIONS ABOUT THIS ANCIENT STATE RUN BY ITS OWN CITIZENS.

Some, like Rousseau, Hegel and other modern "communitarians" think that many of its values and beliefs are exemplary, whereas other "liberals" express grave doubts about its notions of absolute citizenship.

11

Asking Questions

Athenian philosophers were argumentative. They were fascinated by debate and ideas, and invented the subject we now call "philosophy". This means that they were "modern" because they were critical. They refused to accept religious or traditional explanations for anything and asked disturbingly original questions that no one had ever thought of asking before – especially about "society", "morality" and "politics" (which derives from the Greek word *polis*).

The Sophists

Plato (c. 428–347 BC) was the first philosopher to record many of these theoretical discussions about politics. In his book *The Republic*, Socrates, Plato's old teacher and friend, discusses the true nature of "justice" with his Sophist philosopher friends. (This "embedded" word "justice" means something like "behaving as you should".) The Sophists were itinerant, radical thinkers who sold their services as tutors to wealthy families and specialized in teaching rhetoric.

THE SOPHIST THRASYMACHUS BEGINS BY INSISTING THAT ALL GOVERNMENTS ARE FRAUDULENT.

EACH TYPE OF GOVERNMENT ENACTS LAWS THAT ARE IN ITS OWN INTEREST: A DEMOCRACY, DEMOCRATIC LAWS; A TYRANNY, TYRANNICAL ONES; AND SO ON. "RIGHT" IS MERELY THE INTEREST OF THE ESTABLISHED GOVERNMENT.

IN OTHER WORDS, ALL GOVERNMENTS WHO CLAIM A "NATURAL" RIGHT TO RULE ARE ALWAYS DISGUISING THE FACT THAT THEY RULE IN THE INTERESTS OF ONE PARTICULAR GROUP.

PLATO *SOCRATES* *THRASYMACHUS*

Glaucon's View of Society

Another Sophist, **Glaucon**, insists that societies exist only because human behaviour has always to be restrained by law.

Most Sophists insisted that morality, society, the state and governments are always the artificial creations of human beings – there is nothing at all "natural" or "organic" about them.

Beehives and Workers

Plato rejected this subversive scepticism. Both society and the State are natural, inevitable and benign. His mouthpiece "Socrates" rarely engages in real debate, but hammers away constantly at two ideas – that ruling is a **skill**, and that all human beings have a specific and prescribed **natural function**.

> SOME PEOPLE ARE JUST SIMPLY BORN RULERS, AND THE REST OF US MUST REMAIN THEIR OBEDIENT WORKERS!

PERICLES

Plato was a communitarian and his ideal society is like a harmonious beehive in which everybody knows their role, and this is what "justice" or "behaving as you should" is all about.

The Pure Form of the State

Plato was an aristocrat, so his ideal hierarchical society of born rulers and submissive workers isn't much of a surprise. But his advocacy of this orderly beehive rests on more than simple class loyalty. Plato was wholly convinced by the Pythagorean vision of mathematics. Numbers are "pure" – uncontaminated by the world, independent of human desires, eternal, incorruptible and always true. 2+2 will always equal 4, regardless of whether human beings exist or not.

Government by Experts

Plato's idealist metaphysics of "pure Forms" is the result of a whole series of linguistic confusions. It meant that there had to be a perfect "Form" for "The State". His *Republic* is largely concerned with the education of the State's rulers called "The Guardians" – an élite group of political experts who know all there is to know about "The Perfect State", composed of a hierarchy of metals.

This vision of a highly disciplined "command society" has always attracted those whose political instincts are authoritarian. Plato's ideal republic has been condemned for its incipient totalitarianism and praised for its celebration of community values, in more or less equal measure.

Relative Knowledge

We now think that human knowledge is intrinsically fallible and relative. What seems "true" to us about the planets and the stars today will probably seem mostly "false" to us in a few years' time. Citizens of the future may be astonished at the political beliefs we hold now. Philosophers now consider it highly unlikely that there are such things as moral or political "facts", let alone mysterious transcendent "Forms".

So Protagoras the Sophist was probably right to insist that the amateurs of Plato's own democratic Athens had as much right to rule as anyone else.

The Ship of Fools

Plato had an incurable dislike of the Athenian democratic government that had put his teacher, Socrates, to death in 399 BC. In *The Republic* he compares democracy to a ship with a mutinous crew.

But their leader has no knowledge of navigation, the boat goes on the rocks and everyone drowns. Democracy, in other words, is leadership by the stupid, who make unrealizable promises to the ignorant, and this always leads to disaster.

Is Democracy Still Best?

Those who get impatient with the squabbles, delays, horse-trading, populism and general inefficiencies of democracy have often been attracted to the idea of Plato's elitist government. But most of us still think that democracy is a good idea and preferable to all other political ideologies on offer. Plato's analogies are also misleading.

One true mark of a healthy political society may be that its educated citizens engage in debate rather than passively obey orders. Democracies also enable citizens to remove corrupt or incompetent governments, without the need for violent revolution or civil war. But if you think that voters have become directionless consumers influenced by spin-doctors, or feel that politicians are now just populists led by focus groups, then Plato's attacks on democracy might be worth thinking about.

Aristotle and Teleology

Plato's most famous student was the independently minded **Aristotle** (384–322 BC), who disagreed with most of what Plato taught him. Like most ancient Greeks, he believed in "teleological" or "final" causes.

EVERYTHING IN THE UNIVERSE IS DESIGNED FOR A SPECIFIC FUNCTION.

SO, FOR THE GREEKS, THE WORD "GOOD" MEANT SOMETHING LIKE "ACHIEVING ITS PURPOSE".

ORGANIC THINGS CAN LOOK AS IF THEY HAVE A PURPOSE – A "GOOD" OAK TREE IS TALL AND STRONG AND A "GOOD" CAT IS AN EFFICIENT MOUSER.

Darwinists now think this is the wrong way to think about natural objects and causes. Natural objects may **look** perfectly designed, but this is because they have evolved that way, not because there is some mysterious cause pulling them towards perfection. If their environment changed, this would cause or "push" them to change, or face extinction.

The "Good" Man and the Citizen

But, for Aristotle, this comprehensive teleological biology made perfect sense. It meant that human beings could only ever be "good" or happy if they "flourished". So politics needs to be a consequence of **human nature**. Everyone accepts that there are clear criteria we can use to judge whether certain kinds of qualified people, like carpenters and cobblers, are successful.

By examining his fellow humans and himself, Aristotle concluded that the one thing that makes us wholly different from the rest of the natural world is our ability to **reason**. It is that we must cultivate, if we are to reach our inbuilt destiny.

Pragmatic Reason

A "good" or well-functioning human being is one who reacts appropriately ("rationally") to every situation, usually by avoiding extremes of behaviour.

THE FUNCTION OF A MAN IS THE EXERCISE OF HIS SOUL, IN ACCORDANCE WITH A RATIONAL PRINCIPLE. THE FUNCTION OF A GOOD MAN IS TO EXERT SUCH ACTIVITY WELL.

THE BEST SOCIETIES AND STATES ARE THEREFORE "RATIONAL" AND "MODERATE" ONES THAT FOSTER A COLLECTIVE SPIRIT OF MUTUAL CO-OPERATION AND RESPECT.

This means that individuals must think of themselves as citizens first and actively participate in political life, not just passively obey the law. Aristotle's political philosophy isn't exactly startling, but it avoids the utopianism of Plato's *Republic*. If infallible experts do not exist, then politics has to be something rather more pragmatic.

Aristotle's Politics

In *The Politics*, Aristotle recognized that political authority has to depend, to some extent, on the consent of the governed. Since different societies choose different sorts of government, there may not be one "perfect" State. Nevertheless, Aristotle disapproved of oligarchies (rule by the rich) and democracies (rule by the poor).

I FAVOUR A FORM OF "ARISTOCRATIC" RULE BY THOSE BEST QUALIFIED – A SYSTEM WHICH I CALLED "POLITY".

Economic Equality

Aristotle believed that the majority of citizens should be of "middling wealth", so that political equality could not be undermined by economic inequality. Unfortunately, most Athenians would also have agreed with him that slaves were merely fulfilling their "natural" function.

Human Nature and Beliefs

Aristotle was the first philosopher to insist that political life has to be founded on some descriptive account of **human nature**.

EVERY FOOL PRESUMES TO SPEAK AUTHORITATIVELY OF HUMAN NATURE.

BUT THERE ARE LOTS OF DIFFERENT VIEWS ABOUT WHAT HUMAN BEINGS ARE "REALLY LIKE".

YOUR OWN VIEW OF HUMAN NATURE WILL DETERMINE WHAT YOUR ETHICAL BELIEFS ARE AND HOW YOU SHOULD BEHAVE TOWARDS OTHER PEOPLE.

IT WILL PROBABLY INFLUENCE YOUR POLITICAL VIEWS ON HOW SOCIETY SHOULD BE ORGANIZED.

EMMA GOLDMAN (1869–1940)

Your beliefs about yourself and your fellow humans may suggest the **meaning** and **purpose** of human life to you, offer a **remedy** for all that is wrong with the world and may also inspire you with a **vision** of what society should be like.

But your theories and "facts" about human nature are very unlikely to be "value free". They'll be a reflection of your **ideology**.

What are Ideologies?

Ideologies ultimately have a political function. They are normally the beliefs, attitudes and values used to legitimize the power of specific interest groups. They are also usually implicit and "naturalized" so that they remain safely unquestioned.

THE MORE UNEXAMINED THEY ARE, THE MORE POWERFUL THEY TEND TO BE.

THAT IS WHY MOST WESTERNERS TEND "IDEOLOGICALLY" TO HAVE A HIGH REGARD FOR DEMOCRATIC GOVERNMENTS AND CAPITALISM, WHICH THEY THINK OF AS "NATURAL".

The Ideology of Essentialism

The belief that there actually **is** something called "human nature" is now often criticized as "essentialist". If there are some fundamental truths about what people are "really like", then it makes sense to say that these truths should determine how society is organized.

IF, LIKE ME, YOU BELIEVE THAT MOST PEOPLE ARE "ESSENTIALLY" WICKED, THEN YOU'LL BELIEVE IN A REPRESSIVE AND HEAVILY POLICED SOCIETY.

IF YOU ARE ALREADY IN FAVOUR OF AN AUTHORITARIAN SOCIETY, THIS PESSIMISTIC ACCOUNT OF "ESSENTIALLY WICKED" HUMAN NATURE MAKES FOR A GOOD EXCUSE.

How Free Are We?

Theories about human nature also raise metaphysical questions about how free or individual we are in our beliefs and behaviour. Some philosophers suggest that we have no essential human nature but are more like blank sheets of paper "written on" by our social and economic environment. Evolutionary psychologists can be equally determinist when they insist that we are all products of our genetic inheritance.

The Effects of Evolution

Our physical bodies are the result of millions of years of evolution. Evolutionary psychologists suggest that the same is true of our "human nature". We all have certain inbuilt instincts and behavioural traits which are a direct result of our evolutionary past. What especially useful "survival genes" human beings have evolved is not entirely clear. In some non-human animals, aggression is clearly a useful survival mechanism.

Most importantly, however, unlike animals we are not trapped in a routine of unthinking instinctive responses. Human beings can choose to suppress their combative or co-operative instincts.

What Does Evolution Prove?

Comparing ourselves to animals is problematic and potentially misleading because ideology gets in the way.

The anarchist **Peter Kropotkin** (1842–1921) believed that a co-operative society was totally "natural". Rich Victorian industrialists also examined nature, but came to very different and very convenient "Social Darwinist" conclusions.

BEES ARE CO-OPERATORS, SO SOCIABILITY MUST BE THE MAIN FACTOR IN ALL EVOLUTIONARY PROCESSES.

HUMAN ECONOMIC STRUGGLES AND INEQUALITIES ARE AS INEVITABLE AS ALL THE "SIMILAR" ONES OCCURRING IN THE NATURAL WORLD. IT'S QUITE NATURAL FOR US TO BE RICH AND THEM TO BE POOR.

SO, WHAT YOU GET FROM EVOLUTION DEPENDS ON WHAT YOU WANT TO FIND IN IT.

KROPOTKIN

Humans as Selfish Co-operators

It seems unlikely that human beings have survived by constantly fighting each other. It's just as probable that human beings evolved as a successful species because they co-operated. Aristotle seems right to believe that it is as "natural" for gregarious human beings to live in groups as it is for them to have ten toes.

SO, MOST INDIVIDUALS PROBABLY JOIN AND REMAIN IN GROUPS OUT OF ENLIGHTENED SELF-INTEREST – THAT WAY, YOU EAT MORE REGULARLY AND GET PROTECTION FROM ENEMIES.

Human beings usually place a high value on co-operation, generosity and sympathy, and disapprove of more egotistical behaviour. But living in groups can also have the drawbacks of conformity and obedience to tradition. Close-knit communities can stifle individuality, imagination and invention, and worse – encourage hostility to all those perceived as "outsiders".

Game Theory

One way of testing many of these "co-operative" hypotheses about human nature is called "game theory", which seems to show that people are usually nice to each other for selfish reasons. The best way to survive a large number of complex win-or-lose games is to adopt a "Tit-for-Tat" strategy.

YOU BEGIN BY CO-OPERATING WITH EVERYONE AND THEN KEEP DOING SO IF THEY CO-OPERATE WITH YOU.

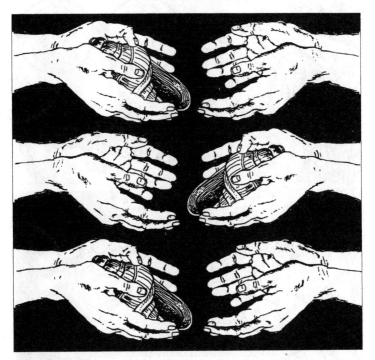

BY ESTABLISHING A SERIES OF LONG-TERM, STABLE AND REPETITIVE RELATIONSHIPS, YOU CAN BUILD UP "POINTS" IN A RELATIVELY STRESS-FREE AND PREDICTABLE WAY.

Reciprocity pays off. But the strategy works only if the games are played by relatively small groups in which each "player" can remember the names and previous behaviour of other players. This may be why Athenian democracy "worked".

Co-operators or Competitors?

Evolutionary psychology and game theory seem to point to certain conclusions that are awkward for those who dream of an ideal utopian society. Humans are complicated beings who are quite prepared to be benevolent, but only if there is some kind of **payback**.

WE MAY BE SELFISH AT HEART, BUT IT IS THAT SAME SELFISHNESS THAT PROVIDES US WITH THE BEST REASON FOR HELPING OTHERS.

BUT UNADULTERATED SELFISHNESS PRODUCES ONLY SHORT-TERM GAINS.

A CAPITALIST SOCIETY THAT ENCOURAGES AND CELEBRATES RAPACIOUS INDIVIDUAL GREED PROBABLY GOES AGAINST WHAT EVOLUTIONARY PSYCHOLOGY TELLS US ABOUT OUR NATURE AS GROUP ANIMALS.

Likewise, a benign but large society that is overburdened with too much government and impersonal bureaucracies may remove from its millions of anonymous members any sense of self-responsibility or reciprocity, and destroy what small sense of community remains.

Who's Right About Human Nature?

The frustrating conclusion is that it is very difficult to know what human nature "really is", and probably impossible to describe it with any degree of objectivity.

Political philosophers will probably always disagree about how static or dynamic, rational or irrational, perfectible or corrupt, self-interested or altruistic we all are. It is not very clear how we can ever judge who is right or wrong about the matter.

Life Without Governments?

States may have little to do with any essentialist models of human nature. Capitalist societies may be a "natural" development from the way we are, but could just as likely be an artificial aberration based on a misleading model of human nature.

> ANARCHISTS SAY THAT HUMAN BEINGS CAN LIVE CO-OPERATIVELY, WITHOUT THE NEED OF STATE COERCION.

> GAME THEORY SEEMS TO SUGGEST THAT ANARCHISTS MIGHT BE RIGHT — PROVIDED THERE AREN'T TOO MANY POWER-HUNGRY INDIVIDUALS, CRIMINALS OR "FREE-RIDERS" AROUND.

> HUMAN BEINGS HAVE, AFTER ALL, LIVED **WITHOUT** GOVERNMENT FOR THOUSANDS OF YEARS MORE THAN THEY'VE LIVED **WITH** IT.

The State is a relatively recent invention. But there are no easy or instant answers. Political philosophy isn't an empirical science. All it can do is clarify and debate these seemingly insoluble problems which always seem to emerge whenever human beings investigate themselves.

Politics After Aristotle

Aristotle was from Macedonia, and it was an invasion from his homeland that finally finished off the Greek City States. A unique kind of political philosophy, which stressed the importance of civic life, disappeared.

NOW IMPERIALISM BECAME THE POLITICAL REALITY IN EUROPE, FIRST WITH ALEXANDER AND THEN WITH THE ROMAN EMPIRE FOR THE NEXT THOUSAND YEARS.

Ancient Anarchists

The philosophers who emerged all over the Hellenistic and Roman worlds – Cynics, Sceptics, Epicureans and Stoics – had little time for political philosophy in a world that now seemed unpredictable and dangerous. The Cynic **Antisthenes** (c. 440–c. 370 BC) was the first Greek anarchist.

I WANT NOTHING TO DO WITH GOVERNMENTS, RELIGION OR PRIVATE PROPERTY.

I AM ANOTHER CYNIC, **DIOGENES** (404–323 BC), AND CLAIM TO BE A "CITIZEN OF THE WORLD".

WE SCEPTICS FINALLY TOOK OVER PLATO'S ACADEMY, BUT HAD LITTLE INTEREST IN POLITICS.

EPICUREANS ARE SENSIBLE ENOUGH TO REALIZE THAT ENGAGING IN POLITICAL DISCUSSIONS IS EXCEEDINGLY RISKY ...

WE RECOMMEND THAT HUMAN HAPPINESS IS SOMETHING THAT CAN NEVER BE FOUND IN POLITICAL LIFE.

Roman Stoics and Early Christians

The most famous Stoic philosophers were the Romans **Seneca** (2 BC–AD 65), tutor to the infamous Emperor Nero, and Emperor **Marcus Aurelius** (AD 121–180).

THE ROMAN EMPIRE IN WESTERN EUROPE COLLAPSED IN THE 5TH CENTURY.

The only civilized discussions about politics took place within the Christian Church, which was established as the official religion of the Roman Empire by Emperor Constantine around AD 320. The Church dominated all intellectual life until the Renaissance of the 15th century.

Christian Dualism

Medieval Christian theologians were pessimistic about human nature and therefore the possibility of any perfectible secular State. Christianity teaches that we are immortal souls, trapped in physical bodies, whose ultimate destiny therefore lies beyond this material plane. It's a very powerful "dualist" model of human beings.

St Augustine's City of God

St Augustine (AD 354–430) lived at a time when Roman civilization was collapsing. Rome was sacked by invading Goths in 410, and many Romans blamed Christians for their apparent lack of interest in the survival of the State. In his book *The City of God*, Augustine attacks the classical Greek idea that human beings are somehow "fulfilled" by living in a rational City State.

> HUMAN BEINGS ARE INTRINSICALLY IRRATIONAL AND VOLATILE. THIS IS WHY GOD HAS SANCTIONED EARTHLY GOVERNMENTS – TO PRESERVE THE PEACE AND ADMINISTER JUST LAWS.

Citizens should obey governments and fight in "just wars". But the true destiny for all human beings lies elsewhere – they are really "citizens of an eternal kingdom" beyond this one.

The Theology of St Aquinas

The Dominican monk in Italy, **St Thomas Aquinas** (1225–74), was rather more optimistic about the State. In his *Summa Theologiae*, Aquinas described all the "Natural" or "Divine" Laws which govern everything in the universe, from gravity to human morality.

I AGREE WITH ARISTOTLE. CHRISTIANS, LIKE ALL HUMAN BEINGS, ARE SOCIAL AND POLITICAL ANIMALS WITH A DESIRE TO LIVE IN SOCIETY.

THE FELLOWSHIP OF SOCIETY BEING NATURAL TO MAN, IT FOLLOWS THAT THERE MUST BE SOME PRINCIPLE OF GOVERNMENT.

As conscious and rational beings, they are able to work out which universal "natural laws" apply to themselves. (These turn out to be mostly about "refraining from harm" and "reciprocity".)

The "positive" or secular laws of the state are derived from natural laws. So, if positive law ever contradicts natural law, then it is invalid and can be disobeyed.

A tyrannical ruler can therefore be justifiably rejected by his people (even though the overthrow of governments usually leads to even greater suffering).

"Natural" Law

Aquinas' idea of "Natural Law" came to dominate much 17th-century political philosophy. Nowadays, we make clear distinctions between the descriptive "laws" of nature and prescriptive laws that are man-made.

WE THINK THERE IS AN OBVIOUS DIFFERENCE BETWEEN SOMEONE "OBEYING" THE LAW OF GRAVITY BY FALLING OFF A CLIFF ...

AND SOMEONE FILLING IN A FORM IN ORDER TO OBEY THE LAWS ON TAXATION.

BUT THE FICTION OF ANCIENT PRE-POLITICAL "NATURAL LAWS" OR "RIGHTS", AS LAID DOWN BY GOD, CAN BE A USEFUL TOOL WITH WHICH TO CRITICIZE TYRANNICAL GOVERNMENTS THAT MISTREAT THEIR CITIZENS.

GALILEO

The Renaissance

That highly complex cultural phenomenon known as the "Renaissance" began in Northern Italy in the 14th century and quickly spread throughout Europe during the following two centuries. It inspired a new spirit of enquiry into all aspects of human life, including politics.

IN THE NEWLY PROTESTANT COUNTRIES OF NORTHERN EUROPE, IT BECAME POSSIBLE TO ARGUE AND DEBATE POLITICAL THEORY MORE OPENLY.

AT LAST WE CAN ASK RADICALLY NEW QUESTIONS ABOUT THE ROLE OF THE STATE AND ITS RELATIONSHIP TO ITS CITIZENS.

ITALY ITSELF WAS DOMINATED BY A FEW POWERFUL CITY STATES LIKE VENICE AND FLORENCE.

Many contemporary inhabitants compared these states to ancient Athens, even though none of them were particularly "democratic". They were ruled either by princes or cabals of rich families. But they did squabble among themselves, just like Athens and Sparta had done.

Machiavelli's Prince

Niccolò Machiavelli (1469–1527) was a practising Florentine politician who did something unusual – he described the behaviour of politicians and wrote about politics as it **is**, rather than prescribing what it **should** be, as nearly all political philosophers had done before and since. His book *The Prince* shocked the whole of Europe and a new word – "Machiavellian" – was used to describe a specific kind of amoral opportunism. His book is about "realpolitik" – the grim reality of everyday political life.

Machiavelli observed what politicians actually **do** – like the infamous Duke Cesare Borgia – and drew some fairly unpalatable conclusions from their behaviour.

State Morality

Wise politicians will lie and break their promises, if it is politically advantageous to do so. Even assassination is justified if it gets results.

And although Machiavelli thought that republics with a measure of popular support were the best form of government, he realized that most people are more interested in security than the morality of their governments.

Cynic or Realist?

Machiavelli saw that it was **power**, exercised with ruthless efficiency, that established and maintained stability and prosperity.

WHETHER MACHIAVELLI IS A "PHILOSOPHER" OR NOT IS DEBATABLE — HIS INTERESTS ARE NOT THOSE OF CONCEPTUAL ANALYSIS.

ABSTRACT THEORIZING IS A WASTE OF TIME! IT ACTUALLY OBSCURES THE REALITIES OF POLITICAL LIFE.

His "infamous" book paved the way for a new kind of political philosophy that had a more cynically realistic view of human nature, and a less idealistic vision of the State and its function.

Hobbes and Cromwell

Thomas Hobbes (1588–1679) was born in the year of the Spanish Armada. He spent most of his life as tutor to the children of the Earls of Devonshire and, as a royalist, had to escape to France to avoid the English Civil War and the rule of **Oliver Cromwell** (1599–1658). Hobbes is often thought of as the first great modern political philosopher.

Like Machiavelli, Hobbes insisted that politics should be removed from religious belief. People always believe in their own interpretation of the Bible, for instance, and are prompted to act from religious conscience. This inevitably leads to extremism and bloody civil war.

The Science of Man

Hobbes was profoundly impressed by geometrical knowledge and how it can be built up deductively from a few elementary axioms. If it worked for mathematics, why not for politics? He began with a completely materialist "science of man".

Human beings are endlessly restless and unstable creatures, pushed in all directions by their appetites and aversions.

Psychological Egoists

Motives and beliefs are the end results of a series of colliding desires and aversions moving around in the mind like restless billiard balls. Human beings are also "rational" in the sense of planning how to satisfy their appetites and think how best to protect themselves from danger. Hobbesian human beings are involuntary "psychological egoists" – utterly selfish creatures programmed to be interested only in their own survival and prosperity.

AND WE ALL KNOW THIS TO BE TRUE ...

WHEN A MAN SLEEPS, HE LOCKS HIS DOORS. DOES HE NOT THERE AS MUCH ACCUSE MANKIND BY HIS ACTIONS AS I DO BY MY WORDS?

The State of Nature

Whenever selfish individuals aggregate, in a pre-social "State of Nature", each one tries to satisfy their own appetite for wealth, friends and reputation, in competition with others. Each individual is also roughly equal in terms of physical strength and intellect. But goods are scarce and violence endemic.

EVERY INDIVIDUAL IS RATIONAL ENOUGH TO REALIZE THAT THE BEST FORM OF DEFENCE IS USUALLY PRE-EMPTIVE ATTACK.

THE END RESULT IS HORRIFIC, FOR EVERYONE …

NO ARTS; NO LETTERS; NO SOCIETY; AND WHICH IS WORSE OF ALL, CONTINUAL FEAR, AND DANGER OF VIOLENT DEATH; AND THE LIFE OF MAN, SOLITARY, POOR, NASTY, BRUTISH AND SHORT.

Hobbes's State of Nature is defined by the lack of all those things that society provides.

The Prisoners' Dilemma

It is a nightmare of violence and insecurity that no one desires but which is the inevitable consequence of each aggressive individual attempting to survive by attacking first.

INDIVIDUALS WILL ACT QUITE RATIONALLY IN ORDER TO PRODUCE A SITUATION THAT NONE OF THEM WANT.

JUST AS INDIVIDUAL FISHERMEN ACT INDEPENDENTLY AND RATIONALLY TO DEPLETE THE OCEANS AND SO DESTROY THEIR LIVELIHOOD.

Political philosophers sometimes call this kind of unwanted end result "The Prisoners' Dilemma" (where it seems quite rational for two prisoners to betray each other, even though the outcome is worse for both of them).

The Way Out

If you accept Hobbes's initial premise about human psychology, then his conclusion is logical. The vicious State of Nature is the chaotic and violent abyss we fall into when there is no sovereign power to impose order.

We can look rationally into the future and see how our personal survival can be assured by agreeing with each other to follow "laws of nature" necessary for self-preservation. Hobbes agrees with St Aquinas that there are "natural laws" – notably the right of every individual to preserve his or her own life, together with a corresponding duty not to injure others.

Enforceable Coercion

There must also be some form of coercive power to punish those who break this "social contract" to their own advantage. *"Covenants, without the Sword, are but Words, and of no strength to secure a man at all."*

> THIS IS HOW IT HAPPENS THAT ISOLATED STRANGERS CAN BECOME SOCIAL BEINGS BY "COVENANT" – AN ENFORCEABLE CONTRACT TO WHICH ALL AGREE.

> HUMAN SOCIETY IS NOT "NATURAL" BUT CONSTRUCTED.

> HUMAN BEINGS ONLY EVER BECOME "SOCIAL" BY AGREEMENT, UNLIKE THE INSTINCTIVE COMMUNITIES OF BEES AND ANTS.

Individuals have to give up their right to govern themselves. A sovereign power is then "authorized" to act for this society of egoistic individuals as a kind of legal fiction which somehow "represents" them all and has absolute power over everybody. This prevents any further conflict. Obedience means protection.

Sovereign Power

The subjects of the sovereign power are "obliged" to obey because they will be forced to do so. Individuals only have the freedom that the sovereign allows them. The sovereign himself does not enter into any kind of contract. If he did so, this would mean that some individuals might question his authority, and so provoke civil war and the return to a "State of Nature".

INDIVIDUALS CAN ONLY EVER REBEL IF THE SOVEREIGN DELIBERATELY SETS OUT TO KILL OR INJURE THEM, AND SO BREAKS THE PRIMARY "NATURAL RIGHT" OF SELF-PRESERVATION FROM WHICH ALL OTHERS ARE DERIVED.

HOW A SOVEREIGN COULD EVER CONSCRIPT AN ARMY IS THEREFORE NOT EXACTLY CLEAR.

Absolute Monarchies

Hobbes begins with free individuals and concludes with sovereignty, which has to be absolute if individuals are to avoid the ever-present threat of political chaos. This absolute sovereign power should be given to a single monarch, because this minimizes the sorts of divisions and corruption that plague all other forms of government.

CHARLES I

HOBBES RELUCTANTLY SUGGESTS THAT "NATURAL LAW" ALSO PLACES A FEW LIMITATIONS ON THE TOTAL AUTHORITY OF ABSOLUTE MONARCHS.

THEY SHOULD APPLY THE LAW UNIVERSALLY AND IMPARTIALLY AND PUNISH INDIVIDUALS ONLY WHEN THERE IS GOOD CAUSE.

But any restrictions on the sovereign's power never become individual citizens' "rights", because these have now all been transferred to the sovereign. (Although how individual rights can be "transferred" or "renounced" isn't always clear, or even necessary.)

Problems with the Hobbesian View

Hobbes's account of human nature, contractual "consent" and political authority has been extraordinarily influential. Contemporary critics were horrified by his cynical definition of human beings and a political philosophy that denied the State any divine sanction. They also saw that there was something "circular" about Hobbes's social contract.

Those who obeyed the contract before the sovereign power was authorized to enforce it would quickly become prey to those who didn't. Hobbes's solution is to make the whole process a kind of instantaneous gamble, made by all parties simultaneously.

Natural Selfishness

Many critics also think that Hobbesian people are strangely atomistic, "ready-made" creatures with no inbuilt sociability. Advocates of "psychological egoism" like Hobbes have great difficulty in trying to redefine words like "generosity" and "altruism" and explain why it is that human beings still regularly approve of such kinds of behaviour.

THE EXISTENCE OF MORAL VOCABULARY IS INEXPLICABLE IF HOBBES'S ACCOUNT OF HUMAN NATURE IS TRUE, BUT QUITE UNDERSTANDABLE IF IT ISN'T.

"HUMAN NATURE" MAY NOT BE AS FIXED AND DETERMINED AS HOBBES INSISTS.

IT SEEMS TO BE MORE MALLEABLE AND SOCIAL THAN HE EVER ALLOWS IT TO BE.

Hobbes cannot allow his egoists to be motivated by anything other than selfishness, because then his "State of Nature" might be something rather less threatening and invalidate the need for absolute sovereignty. Hobbes shows little interest in some sort of intermediate "civil society". His individuals jump from selfish isolationism into a fully formed authoritarian political state.

John Locke

The political philosophy of **John Locke** (1632–1704) probably had more practical influence on historical events and political systems than anything Hobbes wrote. Locke's patron was the famous Earl of Shaftesbury, the principal founder of the Whig party in English politics. Shaftesbury believed in religious toleration and was critical of all forms of absolutism. In 1683 both men had to flee to Rotterdam when Shaftesbury lost his political influence, but they returned in 1688 – the year of "The Glorious Revolution", which replaced the Catholic monarch James II with the Protestant William of Orange.

In the late 1670s, Locke wrote his famous *Two Treatises of Government* in secret and refused to acknowledge it as his own work for many years.

Another State of Nature

Like Hobbes, Locke begins with individuals in a "State of Nature". But Locke's individuals are less psychologically determined or detached. Locke argues that even in this primitive situation, everyone can distinguish between right and wrong.

AN AMERICAN SAVAGE WHO MAKES A PROMISE TO A SWISS GENTLEMAN IN THE BACKWOODS KNOWS THAT PROMISES ARE BINDING.

EVERY INDIVIDUAL IS WELL AWARE OF THE "LAWS OF NATURE", AND OBEDIENCE TO THESE LAWS ENSURES THAT MOST MEN DO NOT HARM THE LIVES, HEALTH, LIBERTY OR PROPERTY OF OTHERS.

Locke's pre-political "community" is essentially a benign version of his own 17th-century society, minus government. It seems quite attractive, but Locke believed that it could only ever be a temporary state of affairs.

Locke's Natural Laws

Locke is more of a traditionalist than Hobbes. He is wisely vague about the origins of "Natural Laws" but insists that they are compulsory because they are God-ordained (which makes God rather like Hobbes's absolute monarch). Natural Laws are also "rational", which makes them universal and absolute.

I THOUGHT I COULD EVENTUALLY PRODUCE A WHOLE MORAL SYSTEM OF "DEDUCTIVE ETHICS" BASED ON "SELF-EVIDENT" NATURAL LAWS FROM SUCH PREMISES AS, "WHERE THERE IS NO PROPERTY, THERE CAN BE NO INJUSTICE."

AND THIS CONCEPT OF "PROPERTY" IS THE KEY TO ALL OF LOCKE'S POLITICAL PHILOSOPHY.

Definition of Property

According to Locke, in the original State of Nature, God gave the Earth to all men. He also gave everyone reason, so that everyone can utilize the world's resources to their best advantage. Everyone owns their own body, so, by mixing the body's labour with nature, individuals acquire property rights over certain bits of land and thereby remove it from the common store.

The Right of Inequality

LOCKE NEVER QUESTIONED SOCIAL INEQUALITY.

IT IS PLAIN THAT THE CONSENT OF MEN HAS AGREED TO A DISPROPORTIONATE AND UNEQUAL POSSESSION OF THE EARTH.

IT'S HARD TO SEE HOW "MIXING" YOUR LABOUR WITH THE LAND GIVES YOU EXCLUSIVE RIGHTS OVER IT.

But what Locke wants to emphasize is that the institution of property existed long before any kind of society or political State came into being. Property ownership gives individuals inviolable rights and freedom from State interference.

The Problem of Vendettas

But even this rather sophisticated State of Nature (that already allows for landed gentry and servant classes) is "inconvenient". A few degenerate individuals will always exist to rob and murder innocent individuals.

EVERY MAN WILL INTERPRET NATURAL LAW DIFFERENTLY, AND SOME MAY EVEN RESORT TO "PRE-EMPTIVE" ACTS OF VIOLENCE THAT HOBBES DESCRIBED.

The Advantages of Society

The solution is to convert the ambiguous diktats of natural law into clearer and enforceable positive law. And this is why individuals first agree to form a contractual "society", but not a State. Society is therefore rather like a joint-stock company that prosperous individuals enter into freely, for reciprocal advantage.

Divine Right

Locke's political philosophy is partly a dialogue with Sir Robert Filmer's *Patriarcha* – a text first published in 1679 which claimed that all sovereigns were sacred persons, divinely appointed, and therefore like fathers given a "natural" authority over their large "family".

But such absolutist views seem impossible to prove, do not explain how it is that successful usurpers inherit divine authority, and, most worryingly, give limitless power to one individual and define all others as "subjects" with no property rights of their own.

Governments and Citizens

Locke's individuals have already made themselves social and do not need an absolute monarch to keep order. All they require is some neutral authority to settle disputes and ensure that criminals are punished "indifferently".

Minimal Government

In a political society, Locke's individuals do not have to give up their rights to life, liberty and property just because a person or institution has been appointed to make law and enforce it. Government is more of a "trustee" than a party to a contract – so it has obligations but no rights. There are also strict limitations placed on government power which depends totally upon the consent of citizens.

So Hobbes uses his State of Nature to show why an absolute sovereignty is necessary; Locke employs his to prove that governments must only ever have limited powers.

Changing Governments

A political society that has neutral judges, a legal framework and an executive with limited powers should be predictable, stable and peaceful. Governments are entrusted with power, but citizens always have the right to remove them if they abuse it – if, for example, they raise taxes against property without consent. If the executive ever becomes tyrannical, then the people may remove it by force.

Rebels and Regimes

Locke considered that a government or monarch would have to be completely oppressive (not just corrupt or mediocre) for this to be a legitimate act. A despotic ruler is best imagined as a "rebel" against political society. An uprising against his authority is merely a way of restoring the political status quo.

Separation of Powers

Locke argued that power should be separated, so that no one political institution has a monopoly. The **Legislative** body makes the laws after due debate and discussion. The **Executive** then carries them out. Locke assumes that the **Judiciary** is part of the Executive.

Who Can Vote?

The role of Locke's government is minimal. The state exists primarily to ensure that there are systematic rules governing the transference of property – and not to redistribute wealth or maintain public welfare.

*ONLY THOSE WHO INHERIT PROPERTY SHOULD HAVE THE VOTE BECAUSE THEY ARE EXPRESSING CONSENT TO A REGIME WHOSE PRIMARY FUNCTION IS TO **PROTECT PROPERTY**.*

THE POOR ARE TOO BUSY WITH THE TASK OF SURVIVING TO EDUCATE THEMSELVES SUFFICIENTLY TO THINK ABOUT POLITICAL MATTERS.

SO WE ARE NOT ENFRANCHISED.

Consent or Subservience

Locke realized that the idea of everyone "consenting" to be ruled by governments was problematic. He agrees that the "consent" of most people is merely "tacit" – citizens are deemed to have agreed to obey the State because they do not emigrate, or because they benefit from all that it provides.

BUT IT IS HARD TO SEE HOW TACIT CONSENT IS MUCH DIFFERENT TO RESIGNATION, SUBSERVIENCE OR INDIFFERENCE.

AND IN A MODERN SOCIETY OF MASS MEDIA, CONSENT CAN SOON BE **MANUFACTURED**.

NOAM CHOMSKY

TRUE CONSENT PROBABLY INVOLVES FREE PUBLIC DEBATE AND SOME ELEMENT OF CHOICE.

Hume's Criticism

In reality, a political system that was truly serious about "consent" would soon become a patchwork quilt of secessionist states. There are also no political states that have ever been founded by hypothetical "contracts", as the Scottish philosopher **David Hume** (1711–76) pointed out. *"If you were to ask most people whether they had ever consented to the authority of their rulers, they would be inclined to think very strangely of you and would reply that the affair depended not on their consent but that they were born to such obedience."*

Citizens must consent to be ruled, and this means continuously and not just at the moment when political society comes into being. There must always be a large area of personal freedom left to each individual and well-defined limits to State power.

Rousseau's Political Philosophy

The political philosophy of **Jean Jacques Rousseau** (1712–78) often follows that of Hobbes and Locke in textbooks on political philosophy.

Civilization and Human Nature

Rousseau was born in the protestant Republic of Geneva, ruled by legislative and administrative assemblies, both composed of ordinary citizens. He was a self-taught scholar of political philosophy and a great admirer of the Greek City States of Athens and Sparta. In 1749, he had a sudden "vision" which made him famous throughout Europe.

I SAW THAT HUMAN BEINGS WERE NOT AS HOBBES OR LOCKE HAD DESCRIBED THEM — PERFECTLY FORMED INDIVIDUALS WITH FIXED CHARACTER TRAITS.

*HUMAN NATURE IS NEVER STATIC BUT EVOLVES ACCORDING TO THE **SORTS OF CIVILIZATIONS** THAT FORM IT.*

Human beings have created unjust and oppressive political States and it is **these** that have made individuals greedy, vicious and "Hobbesian". Most people are alienated from the very institutions they themselves have created.

Pre-social State of Nature

In his *Second Discourse*, Rousseau describes pre-social men and women living in a "State of Nature". But this time they aren't vicious egoists or landed gentry. Rousseau's original humans are equally fictitious but more anthropological.

> IT IS IMPOSSIBLE TO "READ OFF" FROM CORRUPTED MODERN INDIVIDUALS WHAT UNCONTAMINATED PRE-SOCIAL HUMAN BEINGS WERE LIKE …

> ALL ONE CAN DO IS CONJECTURE.

Rousseau's first men and women are only **potential** human beings – isolated, harmless primates who are utterly ignorant of "natural law", even though they instinctively refrain from harming each other.

Property and Law

Then the unfortunate invention of agriculture arrives and is accompanied by the even more disastrous idea of "property" with its corresponding economic inequality. A few clever landowners quickly recognize their need for legitimate and enforceable property rights and so devise the idea of social and political contracts. Everyone who desires peace and security consents to them.

Rousseau does not claim that there is a better "essentialist" human nature that we should all return to, but he does think that the benefits of civilization can only be achieved at the disproportionate cost of a distorted and unnatural humanity.

Natural Education

Rousseau's critique of civilization at first startled and then irritated his fellow Enlightenment "Philosophes", **Voltaire** (1694–1778) and **Denis Diderot** (1713–84). But his "primitivist" philosophy continues to influence all those who think that the price of civilization remains far too high. Fortunately, Rousseau's vision is also more optimistic than it might appear. If human beings have both reason and free will, then it is always possible for them to change their human nature into something more altruistic and collectivist.

IN MY NOVEL **EMILE**, I SUGGEST THAT IT IS POSSIBLE TO EDUCATE A CHILD "NATURALLY", SO THAT HE REMAINS UNCONTAMINATED BY THE EVILS OF CIVILIZATION.

BUT EVEN I MUST EVENTUALLY ABANDON MY SEALED ENVIRONMENT AND INNOCENCE, AND RETURN TO CIVILIZATION — TO BECOME A "GOOD CITIZEN".

Emile must forsake his "natural" self – which makes his unique education seem rather pointless. What needed to change was society itself, and that's what Rousseau's most important political work, *The Social Contract*, is all about.

Freedom and Society

Rousseau realized that children must be socialized if they are ever to become truly human. Human beings function best in families, small groups and as committed citizens of the State. But societies can only come into existence if the behaviour of every individual is restrained by customs, rules and compulsory laws.

The Assembly

Like Hobbes and Locke before, Rousseau accepted the need to explain the moral foundations of political "consent" and "obligation". Hobbes equated sovereignty with an absolute power, separate from the needs and desires of citizens, because the alternative is endless misery. But Rousseau insisted there is a truly moral, and not just a prudential, reason for his citizens to obey the law – because all laws are truly "theirs".

So, paradoxically, in a political society people are more "free". Obedience to society's laws brings everyone more freedom.

The General Will

Since Rousseau's Legislative Assembly involves **all** citizens, the State must remain small – rather like ancient Athens or 18th-century Geneva.

Children are raised to be good citizens who think and behave with a collectivist spirit that soon becomes as natural to them as familial affection. The law and the State are therefore appropriate expressions of the people's will, and this justifies the sovereignty of both.

Perfect Citizens and Backsliders

Erring individuals who disobey the law, ultimately framed for their own benefit, would have to be reminded of their obligations to the State.

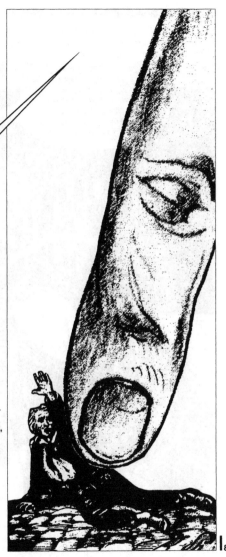

THEY MUST BE FORCED TO BE FREE.

Rousseau's ideal Republic sounds democratic and decent but is founded on very optimistic foundations – perfect citizens expressing some mythical "General Will" for the good of society.

Unlike Locke's landed gentlemen, Rousseau's citizens have no individual rights. The citizens' State has a total monopoly over all political opinion and the absolute power to enforce its will.

The Contract and the Legislator

Rousseau's collectivist State somehow "emerges" from an understanding between primitive individuals in a process that seems more organic than contractual, and so needs a human catalyst in the form of the "Legislator".

Rousseau also recommended that his citizens all agree to a "Civic Religion", a mild form of vague Deism which would nevertheless be compulsory because such a religion would encourage allegiance to the State.

Politics as Ethics

Rousseau's collectivist State is therefore very different from Hobbes and Locke's associations of selfish or property-owning individuals who congregate only for pragmatic reasons of self-interest. For Rousseau, like Plato and Aristotle, politics is a branch of ethics.

This means that abstract entities like Society, the State and the General Will have a unique moral existence of their own, wholly separate from the selfish desires of individuals.

Corsica and Poland

Rousseau's strict communitarianism might appear inconsistent. It came from a man famous for his advocacy of artistic freedom who fled the religious intolerance of his own citizens' Republic of Geneva. However, the advice he gave to the citizens of Corsica and Poland showed that he wasn't a rigid ideologue.

As a lifelong stateless outsider, Rousseau fantasized about a life spent in a small community of like-minded companions. He never completely abandoned his admiration for the Geneva of his childhood.

State Morality

Rousseau's theoretical citizens' State is potentially totalitarian. Recent history seems to show that creating ideal citizens is impossible and probably undesirable. State education in "citizenship" can easily descend into indoctrination. For most ordinary people, loyalty to their oppressive collectivist State is only ever simulated – out of a need for self-preservation.

Rousseau's State has no constitutional checks on its absolute power and fails to recognize individual privacy. His citizens might easily become alienated from the political institutions they themselves have made, a frequent feature of political life that seems inevitable, however hard you try to avoid it.

The French Revolution

The French Revolution began in 1789 with a demand for a more constitutional monarchical government. It ended with the abolition of the monarchy and hereditary aristocracy, the erosion of most formal class distinctions, and the chaotic violence and guillotine of "The Terror". There was now a nation of "equal citizens" with no place for the aristocracy or clergy.

MAXIMILIEN ROBESPIERRE (1758–94), LEADER OF THE RADICAL JACOBINS

THIS NEW EMPIRE OF JUSTICE AND LIBERTY WILL BRING INTO BEING A NEW KIND OF HUMAN BEING AND CITIZENS AT LAST CAPABLE OF CHOOSING THEIR OWN POLITICAL INSTITUTIONS.

BUT MANY REVOLUTIONARY THINKERS FEARED TRUE POPULAR SOVEREIGNTY AND IRRATIONAL MOB VIOLENCE.

THE PHILOSOPHER MARIE-JEAN CONDORCET (1743–94)

DEMOCRACY ONLY PERMITS THE RIGHT TO ELECT A REVOLUTIONARY VANGUARD THAT WILL GIVE THE PEOPLE WHAT IS BEST FOR THEM, AS OPPOSED TO WHAT THEY DESIRE.

LOUIS-ANTOINE SAINT-JUST (1767–94), A LEADING MEMBER OF THE TERROR'S NOTORIOUS "COMMITTEE OF PUBLIC SAFETY"

The Revolution posed new theoretical and practical political problems for which there were no easy or obvious answers. It also gave birth to those early socialists and anarchists, sometimes called "Rousseau's grandchildren".

They had lived through a time of immense revolutionary upheaval and saw how it was possible to change society for ever.

The Birth of French Socialism

Claude-Henri Saint-Simon (1760–1825) (the "father of French Socialism") was convinced that the rigorous application of philosophy and science could solve most social and political problems. By studying the past, one could understand its patterns of evolutionary change – from "organic" feudal states, based on religious superstition, to new secular kinds of "critical" industrial societies ruled by élites of scientists, engineers, and industrialists.

*I RECOGNIZED THE IMPORTANCE OF **CLASS CONFLICT** AS A MAJOR CAUSE OF SOCIAL CHANGE – A MAJOR INFLUENCE ON KARL MARX ...*

THAT'S THE REASON WHY MOST PEOPLE EVER GET TO HEAR OF HIM!

Saint-Simon's socialist vision is of a highly rational and supremely efficient society – a centralized meritocratic beehive guided by technocrats and administrators, and made up of different workers labouring in perfect harmony and solidarity. France would become a vast workshop run by managers, but this time the immense productive potential of science and industry would benefit not just a few entrepreneurs but all the impoverished "industrious classes" that actually create society's wealth.

What is Socialism?

Like all ideologies, socialism comprises arguments, beliefs and ideas about the "true nature" of human beings and the kind of society that best fulfils their needs and desires. It arose in response to industrial capitalism which began to flourish in Europe at the end of the 18th century. Most socialists agree that capitalist societies are deliberately organized so that a small privileged class is always able to exploit the rest. It is only when the working class gains political power that this abuse will end. Individuals have to learn **how** and **why** they are oppressed, in order to change the way things are. One obvious remedy against inequality and poverty is to ensure that the various means of producing wealth (land, machinery and factories) are communally owned. But socialists do not agree about what sorts of "communities" should do the owning.

ALL LABOUR SHOULD BE APPROPRIATELY REWARDED AND ECONOMIC EQUALITY STRIVEN FOR.

HUMAN BEINGS ARE "NATURALLY" HAPPIEST AND MOST FULFILLED WHEN THEY ARE ENGAGED IN SOME FORM OF CREATIVE WORK.

PETER KROPOTKIN
(1842–1921)

MIKHAIL BAKUNIN
(1814–76)

CO-OPERATION RATHER THAN COMPETITION IS THE "NATURAL" STATE OF SOCIETY.

Most liberal philosophers are dubious about socialist ideology. Human beings, they reply, may be "naturally" aggressive, competitive and idle, rather than industrious and co-operative. And a socialist society must be less free because economic equality has to be imposed onto all.

Charles Fourier's Universal Harmony

The eccentric **Charles Fourier** (1772–1837) agreed with Saint-Simon that human history showed the inevitability of enlightenment and progress. Human beings had to progress through 36 different historical periods before they could experience a time of social and political perfection. His most famous work *The Theory of Universal Harmony* is an extraordinary Utopian fantasy proposing communities (or "Phalansteries") of 1,610 people, living communally in one huge building and working each day at 12 different jobs.

AT LEAST, FOURIER EMPHASIZES HAPPINESS AND SPONTANEITY, AND DOES NOT SUBORDINATE THE INDIVIDUAL TO THE STATE.

Owen's Utopian Socialism

Many English writers and philosophers were initially enthralled by events in France but then horrified by the excesses of "The Terror" which gave revolutions a bad name. **Robert Owen** (1771–1858) believed that the social and economic changes he favoured would occur naturally, without any need for violent upheaval.

Owen, the "father of English Socialism", prided himself on being ignorant of most works of political philosophy. He was a manager and then owner of various cotton mills, and a great social reformer. In New Lanark, he devised a model village for the workers at his factories, and made a brief attempt to establish a more radical communitarian society in New Harmony, Indiana.

Small-scale Democracies

Owen was also closely involved with both the co-operative and trade-union movements in Britain. In *A New View of Society*, he firmly agreed with Rousseau that human beings are determined by social, educational and economic circumstances – the poor are rarely poor because they are idle or feckless.

Owen had his own unique vision of a future society – small-scale self-governing communities of workers and families owning all the means of production. Only such small self-supporting communities could ever be truly democratic. Eventually, when the whole world consisted of federations of agricultural and industrial communities, the need for governments and States would disappear.

Anarchism

Anarchism is the other great political ideology fathered by the French Revolution. Anarchist ideology has much in common with socialism but firmly believes that individuals and societies can be organized without any need for state coercion. Societies are natural but states are artificial impositions. **William Godwin** (1756–1836) was inspired by the Revolution to write his book *Enquiry Concerning Political Justice* (1793) in which he argued for a stateless society. Some other key anarchists are **Pierre Proudhon** (1809–65), **Mikhail Bakunin** (1814–76) and **Peter Kropotkin** (1842–1921).

ALL ANARCHISTS REJECT THE AUTHORITY OF GOVERNMENTS (EVEN SOCIALIST ONES) AND CLASSICAL LIBERAL ARGUMENTS FOR THEIR LEGITIMACY.

POWER OF ALL KINDS IS ALWAYS ABUSED AND INEVITABLY RESULTS IN COERCION AND OPPRESSION.

LIKE MANY SOCIALISTS, WE LOOK TO THE END OF CAPITALISM.

BUT LIKE LIBERALS, WE ARE PROFOUNDLY SUSPICIOUS OF STATE POWER.

Anarchists envisage a future society free of exploitation and inequality, and somehow more "rational" or "natural" than any that now exist. Personal freedom would be maximized, material goods fairly distributed, and governments would cease to exist.

Liberty Without Property?

How this attractive state of affairs can be achieved, however, is a problem that has always divided anarchists because they give different accounts of human nature, the altruism of which it is capable and therefore of the forms of economic life appropriate to such beliefs.

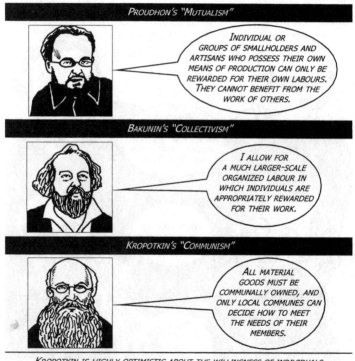

PROUDHON'S "MUTUALISM"

INDIVIDUAL OR GROUPS OF SMALLHOLDERS AND ARTISANS WHO POSSESS THEIR OWN MEANS OF PRODUCTION CAN ONLY BE REWARDED FOR THEIR OWN LABOURS. THEY CANNOT BENEFIT FROM THE WORK OF OTHERS.

BAKUNIN'S "COLLECTIVISM"

I ALLOW FOR A MUCH LARGER-SCALE ORGANIZED LABOUR IN WHICH INDIVIDUALS ARE APPROPRIATELY REWARDED FOR THEIR WORK.

KROPOTKIN'S "COMMUNISM"

ALL MATERIAL GOODS MUST BE COMMUNALLY OWNED, AND ONLY LOCAL COMMUNES CAN DECIDE HOW TO MEET THE NEEDS OF THEIR MEMBERS.

KROPOTKIN IS HIGHLY OPTIMISTIC ABOUT THE WILLINGNESS OF INDIVIDUALS TO HAVE NO PROPERTY OF THEIR OWN AND TO WORK WITHOUT MATERIAL INCENTIVES OF ANY KIND.

Some anarchists are right-wing libertarians who reject any State interference in the affairs of the individual – even if this means that powerful capitalists will flourish at the expense of everyone else.

Anarchist Social Morality

Those very few short-lived anarchist societies have usually been violently suppressed – for instance, by Spanish Fascism in the Civil War of 1936–9 and Russian Bolshevism in 1921. But anarchist ideology itself seems unlikely to disappear. It is a useful corrective to authoritarian aspects of socialist ideology and has contributed greatly towards modern feminist theory and practice. Various direct-action campaigns, like the current movement against global capitalism, are "anarchist inspired".

Quite what a "natural society" without governments would be like is anyone's guess. So again, as always, political ideology depends on the even more speculative one about the "true nature" of human beings.

Hegel's Political Philosophy

Georg Wilhelm Friedrich Hegel (1770–1831) was a professional academic for most of his life and an employee of the Prussian state.

Hegel agreed that civil society and the State were more or less the same thing and, like Rousseau, rarely made much distinction between them. For Hegel, the State is an ethical entity with a unique identity of its own, not just an artificial legal arrangement made by individuals striving to protect their own interests.

The Philosophy of Right

Like most political philosophers, Hegel tries to reconcile subjective individuals, and their specific interests, with their equal need for objective social and political institutions.

It is a complicated and lengthy interactive process which Hegel explores at length in *The Philosophy of Right*.

Hegel begins by pointing out that human beings are social animals defined by their relation to others.

Adult individuals have a greater sense of their own unique identity, are also driven by self-interest and a desire to accumulate property, so their relationships with others are primarily economic. But a market economy needs to be controlled by a legal system so that exchange is well regulated. And, according to Locke, that is more or less how the State begins and its function ends.

Citizens and the Organic State

Hegel's State has to be much more than just a regulatory body. It is not a product of contractual negotiations but the organic and inevitable consequence of how human beings are. It is therefore the destiny of human beings to develop within States. The State has an ethical dimension beyond the self-interest of its individual members.

THE STATE IS ALMOST AN EXTENSION OF "FAMILY", BECAUSE IT DEMANDS A SIMILAR MEASURE OF ALTRUISTIC BEHAVIOUR AND SOLIDARITY AMONG ITS CITIZENS.

IT EXPECTS THEM TO FIGHT IN ITS DEFENCE AND TO PAY TAXES TO SUPPORT ITS WEAKER MEMBERS.

And States don't just control civic society – they constitute it. They make "rational freedom" possible for all. Being a part of the State also changes the consciousness of each individual – how they think about themselves and each other.

The Constitution

Citizenship of a modern State creates more individual freedom than was ever possible within the ancient Greek Polis. Individuals can pursue their own interests in various economic, cultural and religious activities, as well as participating in social and political life.

> THE STATE MAKES POSSIBLE BOTH THE MAXIMUM SATISFACTION OF THE INDIVIDUAL'S PARTICULAR WANTS AND NEEDS **AND** THE REALIZATION OF ONE'S ESSENTIAL NATURE AND TRUE FREEDOM.

Hegel's ideal political society consists of an Assembly of States in which different elements of society have a say in the legislature and political decision making. An upper echelon of professional civil servants (the "universal class") ensures that no one interest group comes to dominate. Rather like Plato's Guardians, this élite group is appointed on merit and is extremely powerful.

The All-Powerful State

Hegel's political structure is headed by a hereditary monarch, a symbolic figure who embodies the unity of the State. Its framework of checks and balances is conservative, traditional and very similar to the constitutional monarchy of Hegel's own 19th-century Prussia. Hegel's feelings about his State are sometimes rather alarming.

Hegel is often accused of being the servile prophet of Prussian nationalism, even though he was in favour of a constitutional monarchy with a well-defined separation of powers, codified law, jury systems and freedom of speech and opinion.

Hegel's Metaphysics

Like many other political philosophies, Hegel's is founded on an extremely elaborate metaphysics of philosophical idealism, theories about the evolution of human consciousness, and a profoundly historicist vision of human progress. Aristotle maintained that reason was the defining characteristic of human beings.

Hegel was convinced that history is essentially the evolutionary and progressive narrative of this collective human consciousness, a mysterious entity he called "Spirit". Individual minds are therefore all part of the one universal mind that determines all that is "real" for human beings.

The Dialectic

Human consciousness is never static but constantly evolving more productive conceptual frameworks which stem from the absorption of older, less adequate ones. New experiences can be structured appropriately in progressive stages.

*HUMAN CONSCIOUSNESS EVOLVES BY **CONFLICTS** AND **RESOLUTIONS** ...*

HUMAN BEINGS DON'T JUST APPREHEND THE WORLD BUT MANIPULATE AND CHANGE IT.

Constant changes in history mean that there must always be a battle between different political ideas in a uniquely Hegelian "logical" process known famously as the "dialectic". Opposing political theories inevitably enter a complex operation of mutual assimilation (or "synthesis") to produce yet more progressive notions of the State, citizenship and freedom.

Rational Freedom and Progress

This dialectical process means that human beings will eventually achieve an awareness of the necessity for "rational freedom" – the synthesis between abstract limitless freedom and the demands of social and political life.

Hegel concludes that human beings are necessarily **state creatures** destined to develop within political communities. States are the inevitable result of us being the sort of gregarious, freedom-loving creatures that we are.

States and citizens together will grow increasingly more rational as the whole teleological process advances through time.

telos, from the Greek, "goal" or "aim" – **teleological**, "goal-directed"

Criticism of Hegel's State

Hegel's attempts to make the State a logical and ethical offshoot of an evolving human consciousness has not gone unquestioned. Not many philosophers now accept the core "theological" doctrines of Hegelianism – especially his account of "Spirit" as divine universal mind – and not many now believe in his progressive, teleological and historicist account of human consciousness, societies and states.

He also thought that some more "evolved" states had the "right" to dominate others. And, like Locke, Hegel's citizens are all property owners who have "objectified" their "subjective" desires and so gained a recognized place within society.

Nevertheless, Hegel's political philosophy is a serious attempt to show how the modern State can mould self-centred, acquisitive market-economy individuals into communal and altruistic citizens. Obedience to his Ethical State is a **disposition**, more than just a matter of convenience. And this could be both an admirable and a very dangerous idea.

Edmund Burke's Conservatism

Like other late-18th-century political conservatives, Hegel was shocked by the extremism and violence of the French Revolution. *The Philosophy of Right* was to some extent written as a reaction to those events. He distrusted revolutionary fervour of all kinds and was mostly hostile towards the military might and expansionist ambitions of the Napoleonic regime. Similar reservations were uttered by the voice of English conservatism, **Edmund Burke** (1729–97).

LIKE HEGEL, I BELIEVE THAT THE STATE IS AN EVOLVING HISTORICAL PHENOMENON, SIMILAR TO A COMPLEX LIVING ORGANISM.

ITS COMPLEXITY IS HELD TOGETHER BY A MIXTURE OF WRITTEN RULES AND UNWRITTEN CUSTOMS, ADHERED TO, USUALLY UNTHINKINGLY, BY ITS CITIZENS.

PREJUDICE RENDERS A MAN'S VIRTUE HIS HABIT.

It is this instinctive "prejudice" that holds societies together and makes individuals into citizens, far more than any conscious adherence to moral or political principles.

Burke's conservatism is the product of his epistemological scepticism. Because society as a whole is infinitely complex and extremely subtle, no one individual can fully comprehend it. It is therefore dangerous to reject traditional political and social institutions in favour of some abstract Utopian alternative founded on vague concepts like "natural rights".

In *Reflections on the Revolution in France* (1790), he criticized the French for destroying the political and social institutions that made civilized life possible. The British had been able to change their king in 1688 without destroying their stable political regime. Burke is an "anti-philosopher" – distrustful of abstractions and lofty ideals – who warns his fellow citizens of the dangers of revolutionary thought and practice. (His own conservative political views are, of course, wholly ideological.)

Paine's Rights of Man

Burke's views were attacked by another Englishman, **Thomas Paine** (1737–1809), author of *Rights of Man*. Paine emigrated to America in 1775 where he wrote *Common Sense* in support of the American Revolution. He then visited France in 1787 and was elected to the National Assembly.

In later works, like *Agrarian Justice*, Paine argued for some kind of welfare state and redistributive taxation. Paine was a great polemicist who defended ordinary people's right to debate political principles and agitate for reforms.

The Human Rights Issue

Paine was responsible for popularizing the idea of "human rights" which has worried political philosophers ever since. "Rights" are usually claimed by the weak against the powerful. Governments are reluctant to accede to demands for them which often become expensive obligations – "rights" to childcare, education, healthcare and so on.

LEGAL OR POSITIVE RIGHTS ARE EASY TO EXPLAIN – A BODY OF PEOPLE AGREE, PERHAPS CONTRACTUALLY, TO AWARD LEGALLY ENFORCEABLE PRIVILEGES TO EACH OTHER, AND THAT'S THAT …

NO! THE LAW IS ONLY CODIFYING "NATURAL" OR "MORAL" RIGHTS THAT ALREADY EXIST.

BUT HOW CAN RIGHTS EVER BE "NATURAL" OR "SELF-EVIDENT"?

IF RIGHTS CORRESPOND TO THE MOST ELEMENTARY FACTS OF HUMAN NATURE, THEN MAYBE THEY **DO** PRE-DATE SOCIETY AND GOVERNMENTS.

BUT SUCH CLAIMS ARE DIFFICULT, IF NOT IMPOSSIBLE, TO PROVE.

WHEN DIFFERENT "RIGHTS" COME INTO CONFLICT, HOW DO WE KNOW WHICH ONE TAKES PRIORITY?

Right and Left Hegelians

Hegelian political philosophy was adopted by German "Right Hegelians" who thought that the Prussian State had more or less reached the final dialectical stage of perfect rationality and should remain unaltered. "Left Hegelians" thought that the Hegelian process still had a long way to go. Who can now remember the names of the former? But everyone has heard of the most famous Left Hegelian – **Karl Marx** (1818–83).

I AGREE WITH HEGEL THAT SOCIETIES ARE LIKE ORGANISMS – ALWAYS "EVOLVING" FROM PRIMITIVE TO MORE ELABORATE FORMS.

THIS LENGTHY EVOLUTIONARY PROCESS IS ASSUMED TO END IN THE PERFECTIBILITY OF BOTH HUMAN BEINGS AND THEIR SOCIETIES ...

... BY PROGRESSING THROUGH CONTRADICTIONS.

To begin with, Marx agreed with Hegel – it was the incessant war between **ideas** that determined human consciousness and history.

Economic Determinism

But then Marx famously discovered that Hegel "stood on his head" and had to be "turned upside down". What Marx meant was that ideas cannot determine human reality but – the other way round – that objective material forces and economic realities are what determine human ideas. This is why Marx is familiarly known as a "dialectical materialist".

ECONOMIC DETERMINISM

OBJECTIVE MATERIAL FORCES

ECONOMIC REALITIES

HUMAN IDEAS

*IT IS NOT THE CONSCIOUSNESS OF MEN THAT DETERMINES THEIR BEING BUT, ON THE CONTRARY, THEIR **SOCIAL BEING** THAT DETERMINES THEIR CONSCIOUSNESS.*

Marx's political philosophy, although complex and wide-ranging, rests on this relatively simple premise of **economic determinism**. Human beings are best defined not as selfish egoists but as economic beings who struggle to produce material goods from their physical environment. Emancipation comes from a full understanding of economics and its production of social relations, not through the mystical evolution of some absolute consciousness.

The Inevitability of Capitalism

Marx believed that economics could be made "scientific" in the same way that Darwin had made biology into "science" – by subjecting all natural phenomena to determinist evolutionary laws. The scientific study of economics and its history revealed the elemental causes of all human beliefs and activities.

THE ECONOMIC "SUBSTRUCTURE" ALWAYS DETERMINES THE "SUPERSTRUCTURES" OF ALL POLITICAL, RELIGIOUS AND CULTURAL PHENOMENA.

Most classical economists before Marx, like **Adam Smith** (1723–90) and **David Ricardo** (1772–1823), had assumed that capitalism was inevitable, even God-inspired. Locke took for granted the belief that property and capitalism were as "natural" as society itself. Rousseau had challenged this assumption, and Marx insisted that property and its monstrous child, capitalism, were unnatural, unjust and eventually doomed.

Wicked Capitalists

But what is capitalism? Throughout history, human beings have engaged in varieties of economic activity through different "means of production". Capitalism was a relatively recent form of economic activity which proved extremely successful in producing large amounts of material goods. The owners of capital had benefited massively from the efficiencies of the Industrial Revolution which exploited the "assembly line" division of labour in a highly disciplined factory system.

Capitalism was profoundly unjust because the means of production was owned by a wealthy few. A large proportion of the population was now factory workers, treated like machines – a means to someone else's economic end.

Congealed Labour

Marx agreed with Ricardo's "labour theory of value" that capitalists made their profits and increased their capital **from their employees**. So their wealth is really "congealed labour".

Capitalism also means that employees are "alienated" from the goods they spend most of their time producing ...

... alienated from each other as workers, from a society that is not "theirs" and, most of all, from their own true human potential.

For Marx, modern society was little more than an unequal marketplace, held in check by State power, itself devised by the rich few to coerce everybody else. Hegel had maintained that the State was an inevitable and organic offshoot of rational human nature. Marx viewed it as a capital-producing conspiracy.

The Function of Ideologies

It isn't just brute coercion that maintains capitalist society. The subtler power of ideology was even more important. Human beings conceive of the world in irrepressibly mythical ways. They impose categories onto their experiences to make sense of them. These categories can be metaphysical, political, ethical or religious.

MOST PEOPLE SUFFER FROM "FALSE CONSCIOUSNESS" — THEY ACCEPT AS "NATURAL" THOSE ATTITUDES, VALUES AND BELIEFS THAT BENEFIT ONLY ONE PARTICULAR CLASS ...

THE IDEAS OF THE RULING CLASS ARE IN EVERY EPOCH THE RULING IDEAS.

PEOPLE BELIEVE THAT CERTAIN POLITICAL AND ECONOMIC PRACTICES ARE UNIVERSALLY BENEFICIAL, WHEN THEY ARE NOT.

We accept the need for stringent property laws, strong governments, an established church and capitalist economics, because we are encouraged to think that these institutions benefit all, rather than just the rich few. Our "majority" values, beliefs and attitudes are not really our own.

The Spectre of Communism

But Marx was also an optimist. Because history is relentlessly dialectical, this means that present inequalities and injustices of the capitalist system will eventually be challenged.

PHILOSOPHERS HAVE ONLY INTERPRETED THE WORLD, IN VARIOUS WAYS; THE POINT, HOWEVER, IS TO *CHANGE* IT.

In the famous *Communist Manifesto*, Marx explains how capitalism contains the seeds of its own destruction. As all economic power is concentrated in fewer and fewer hands, the impoverishment of most working people must relentlessly continue. This meant that a future dialectical conflict would inevitably occur between two classes – the small but dominant bourgeois class of factory-owners and the huge, but pauperized, proletarian class of wage-earners.

The Radiant Future

A workers' revolution would be inevitable, not necessarily because of proletarian fervour but because of the doomed resistance of the bourgeoisie to the inescapable forces of history – given a helping hand from a few committed Communist revolutionaries.

CLASS STRUGGLE WOULD END, AND, AFTER A BRIEF DICTATORSHIP OF THE PROLETARIAT, THE STATE WOULD "WITHER AWAY".

Marx's final Utopian vision is one of a Communist society to which individuals contribute according to their abilities and receive according to their needs. Human beings would no longer be dominated by capitalist self-interest but would live in a rational society in which property, state-coercion and the artificially created scarcity of essential goods would no longer exist.

Fact or Prophecy?

Marxism is both a detailed "scientific" analysis of the economics of capitalism and an idealistic plea for the sort of socialist utopias imagined by the French political activists Fourier and Saint-Simon, themselves the "grandchildren of Rousseau". But a century and a half later, capitalism still seems to be thriving.

Nowadays most Marxists think that the relationship between economics and human social, cultural and political life is rather more complicated. Many political ideas seem to have a life of their own, independent of
economic causes.

Class and the State

Marx's definition of "class" is also problematic and his remarks about its relation to the state, fragmentary and confused. It's not always clear if states arise **because** of class division or are the **cause** of it. Not everyone can be neatly catalogued as a member of one specific class, and not all classes are always economically and politically unequal.

But positive laws, customs, ethical rules and even states seem to be more fundamental than, and so prior to, any systematic economic activity like capitalism.

A Stateless Society

Nevertheless, for Marx, it followed that when any society became "classless", the state itself would "wither away". Like Rousseau, Marx thinks that all social ills could be rationally solved by adjusting social conditions. But even a classless society of decentralized communes would probably need some central agency to enforce rules and contracts and to resolve conflicts between different group interests.

ANY COMPLEX INDUSTRIAL SOCIETY WILL NEED A MANAGERIAL CLASS WITH SOME DEGREE OF AUTHORITY, HOWEVER MUCH IT IS UNDER WORKERS' CONTROL.

BUT THERE WOULD NO LONGER BE ANY NEED FOR THE ORGANIZED POWER OF ONE CLASS TO SUPPRESS EVERYONE ELSE.

Marx's communards would be without property, immune from material wants and no longer ignorant about the economic basis of society. "Politics" as we now understand it would come to an end because it would no longer have any obvious function.

Revolution Delayed

Marxism has had a huge influence on political philosophy, if not for its Utopian elements. Capitalism and its child, the modern state, both seem to have put off the day of reckoning by smoothing out the cruelties of the capitalist system – with increasingly large doses of social welfare, legitimized trade unionism, redistributive taxation and other kinds of social intervention. Nevertheless, political philosophers of all varieties have, and always will find, Marxism invaluable for the conceptual tools it provides in its analysis of the fundamental nature of capitalism and its complex relationship to the modern state.

Developments of Marxism

Marxist philosophy was developed in Germany in the 1920s and 30s by the "Frankfurt School" philosophers **Theodor Adorno** (1903–69), **Herbert Marcuse** (1898–1979) and others who fled to America in the following decade. They re-emphasized the power of ideology to delude and control all those who benefit least from a hierarchical capitalist society.

> IT IS THEREFORE VITAL THAT ORDINARY PEOPLE FREE THEMSELVES FROM OPPRESSIVE INSTITUTIONS AND GRASP THE POSSIBILITIES OF AN ALTERNATIVE SOCIETY, FREE OF DOMINATION, IF TRUE HUMAN POTENTIAL IS EVER TO BE ACHIEVED.

Adorno came pessimistically to believe that ideological indoctrination was so embedded it was virtually impossible to change modern capitalist societies.

Marcuse introduced Freudian terminology into his Marxist discourse. Words like "sane" and "neurotic" became politicized and socially analytic.

Marcuse concluded that advanced industrial modes of production inevitably create rigidly conformist and closed societies of all political types. And these can only exist because of an even more excessive "surplus repression".

Gramsci's Theory of Hegemony

The Italian philosopher **Antonio Gramsci** (1891–1937) concluded that orthodox Marxism underestimates the ideological power of "bourgeois myths" in the socialization process.

> MOST PEOPLE ACCEPT THE IDEAS THAT ARE SOCIALLY "IN PLACE" …

> THIS UNTHINKING ACQUIESCENCE MAINTAINS THE HEGEMONIC SUPREMACY OF THE RULING CLASSES FAR MORE EFFICIENTLY THAN SPECIFIC MEANS OF PRODUCTION.

The dominant capitalist "hegemony" persists unchallenged – and averts revolution – because of the uncritical acceptance of bourgeois values rather than through any overt use of force. Marxists after Marx get more Hegelian in their insistence that it is ideas, and not just brute economics, that form human reality and reinforce political orthodoxies.

Our Political Ideology

The dominant political ideology of the West is known as "Classical Liberalism". One historian, **Francis Fukuyama** (b. 1952), recently and famously maintained in his book *The End of History and the Last Man* (1989) that, with the collapse of all socialist alternatives to Western liberal democracy, classical liberalism has triumphed.

POLITICAL HISTORY HAS FINALLY REACHED SOME KIND OF CONCLUSION.

IT IS A HEGELIAN VIEW THAT HAS NOT GONE UNCHALLENGED, EVEN THOUGH MOST OF US IN THE WEST ASSUME THAT OUR POLITICAL BELIEFS AND VALUES ARE NORMAL, OBVIOUS AND UNIVERSAL.

WHEN, OF COURSE, THEY ARE RELATIVE AND HISTORICAL.

JACQUES DERRIDA

It is often difficult for us to "see" our own ideology, because it is so deeply rooted in our culture and vision of the world. Capitalist economics now seems wholly "natural" to us because we have never known anything else.

Origins of Liberalism

"Classical Liberalism" has its origins in the 17th-century philosophies of Hobbes and Locke. Like all political ideologies, it is founded on a model of human nature. It claims that human beings are not naturally co-operative or altruistic, but are rational beings, determined to maximize their own economic interests.

THE STATE EXISTS MERELY TO ENSURE THAT INDIVIDUALS ARE PROTECTED FROM EACH OTHER.

ITS ROLE IS NOT TO PURSUE "THE COMMON GOOD" OR ADVOCATE SOME TELEOLOGICAL "GOAL" MODEL OF HUMAN NATURE.

THIS MEANS THAT THE STATE HAS NO RIGHT TO INTERFERE IN ANY INDIVIDUAL'S PRIMARY RIGHTS OF FREEDOM AND PROPERTY.

"Society" is envisaged as an aggregate of individuals. The role of the State is primarily regulatory, not constructive. So classical liberalism is a curious ideology because it is both a theory of the state and a theory that rejects it.

The Marketplace

Classical liberalism happily accepts that society is a **marketplace**. The economist **Adam Smith** (1723–90) was the first to recognize what this means – a collection of private individuals motivated by self-interest make, buy and sell goods, which, miraculously, then has the net effect of making society as a whole more prosperous.

It is therefore unwise for the State to interfere with this magical process, and pointless, or even counterproductive, to try to make individuals more philanthropic or co-operative.

Free Enterprise and Equality

Another ideological myth of liberalism is that every individual is economically "equal". Human life in a capitalist society may be competitive and involve ruthless evolutionary economic struggle, but the outcomes are fair, because everyone has had the "equality of opportunity".

THIS MEANS THAT INEQUALITIES ONLY EVER REFLECT INDIVIDUAL EFFORT AND ENTITLEMENT.

In a liberal meritocratic society, the most deserving are rewarded, and the successful benefit everyone by creating wealth which "trickles down" to the less fortunate. So "Justice" is about ensuring that individuals can pursue their desires without hindrance – not about attempting to distribute goods fairly.

Contracts, Constitutions and Tolerance

Liberalism also insists that the state can only ever hold power on trust, must rely on the consent of the people and must be subject to a "contract". As the franchise has become more extensive and virtually universal, consent nowadays gets linked more to the idea of a majority vote, which somehow gives governments a mandate to act as they see fit.

ANY EXCUSE! BUT EVEN DEMOCRATICALLY ELECTED GOVERNMENTS CANNOT HAVE ABSOLUTE POWER.

THEIR POWERS MUST BE RESTRAINED BY A CONSTITUTION AND THE LAW WHICH TOGETHER ENSURE THAT INDIVIDUAL FREEDOMS ARE NOT UNDULY IMPEDED.

FRANKS PRETZELS SODA JUICE CHIPS

GEORGE WASHINGTON

Liberalism also makes reciprocal tolerance a virtue. No one has a monopoly over the truth. Individuals must be allowed to worship how they wish, have their own political opinions, *and* be tolerant of others with views different from their own.

What is the Use of Voting?

One consequence of liberal ideology is that unimpeded free "citizens" have very little real political power. Individuals have the right to vote in elections at regular intervals for governments which are then only responsible to their electorates in a fairly minimal sense.

The Distribution Problem

But merely regulating and harmonizing the private interests of the marketplace does not, in practice, seem to produce the good of all. In any economically competitive society, there will be losers.

And this is where the advocates of liberalism start to disagree with each other.

Unrestrained capitalism might be economically efficient but certainly does produce extremes of wealth and poverty which can destabilize society. Most contemporary Western governments treat citizens humanely, if not equally, by intervening in capitalist economics and moderating its excesses. It is this "distribution problem" that has dominated political philosophy in recent years.

Bentham's Utilitarianism

If the state must refrain from imposing models of human nature or society onto an unaligned collection of individuals, then how can it decide on policy? The answer was provided by the English Utilitarian philosopher **Jeremy Bentham** (1748–1832) in his book *An Introduction to the Principles and Morals of Legislation*. Bentham was leader of a group called "The Philosophical Radicals" who were interested in the liberal reform of the law and all public institutions.

BENTHAM DECLARED THAT THERE IS ONLY ONE ELEMENTARY AND INCONTESTABLE TRUTH ABOUT HUMAN BEINGS ...

NATURE HAS PLACED MANKIND UNDER THE GOVERNANCE OF TWO SOVEREIGN MASTERS, **PAIN** AND **PLEASURE**. IT IS FOR THEM ALONE TO POINT OUT WHAT WE OUGHT TO DO, AS WELL AS TO DETERMINE WHAT WE SHALL DO.

And this primitive fact about human beings forms the basis of all "Utilitarian" political and moral philosophy.

Bentham agreed with Hobbes that human beings are innately selfish – they have to be, in order to survive. Like all sentient organisms, they advance towards pleasure and retreat from pain. Government policy and legislation should reflect this biological and psychological fact.

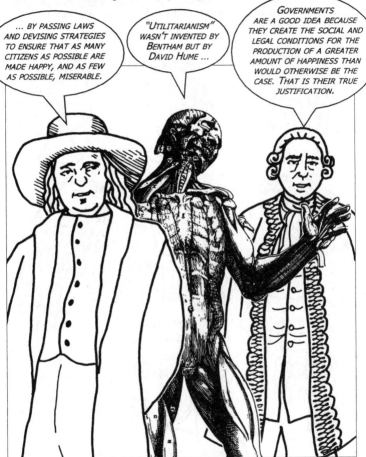

… BY PASSING LAWS AND DEVISING STRATEGIES TO ENSURE THAT AS MANY CITIZENS AS POSSIBLE ARE MADE HAPPY, AND AS FEW AS POSSIBLE, MISERABLE.

"UTILITARIANISM" WASN'T INVENTED BY BENTHAM BUT BY DAVID HUME …

GOVERNMENTS ARE A GOOD IDEA BECAUSE THEY CREATE THE SOCIAL AND LEGAL CONDITIONS FOR THE PRODUCTION OF A GREATER AMOUNT OF HAPPINESS THAN WOULD OTHERWISE BE THE CASE. THAT IS THEIR TRUE JUSTIFICATION.

Hume also maintained that, although it was impossible to *prove* any moral or political ideas, that shouldn't prevent us from following those we preferred.

A Science of Morals

Bentham was an atheist who recommended religious tolerance, a republican who respected the desires of the royalist majority, and a committed democrat. His philosophy was initially inspired by the chaos of the English legal system which, as a lawyer himself, he saw as being based on a hotchpotch of tradition, precedent and prejudice.

Bentham was dismissive of all moral systems that were not as "scientific" as his own, especially those based on unquestioned beliefs in "Natural Law" and "Natural Rights".

The Free-Enterprise Market

Governments that adhere to Utilitarian principles determine social policy by stimulating the production of "The Greatest Happiness" and distributing it to "the greatest number" possible. Like Adam Smith, Bentham was convinced that capitalism was the only practical way of creating wealth and happiness.

Calculating Consequences

Utilitarianism is odder than it at first appears. It is a materialist philosophy that makes no appeals to "reason" or other transcendent foundations. Bentham believed that human happiness could be measured scientifically and accurately with something he called "felicific calculus". This quantifies the intensity, duration and reliability of happiness and the extent to which it can be distributed.

The legal punishment of felons is justifiable, not because the State requires retribution, but because such punishments act as a deterrent on other would-be future criminals.

Useful to Government Policy

Utilitarianism can be made into a moral guide for individuals. But it is a political philosophy helpful mostly to liberal governments trying to frame domestic policies.

Blind Spots of Utilitarianism

Critics of Utilitarianism argue that its materialist approach undervalues the complexity of human nature. Human beings are intellectual and spiritual beings, as well as pleasure-seekers. Human happiness is subjective, relative and so impossible to quantify. Utilitarianism is also wrong to dismiss motives as irrelevant. Future consequences are not always predictable in the long run. Utilitarianism can also sanction the breaking of traditional moral rules, if, by so doing, greater happiness results.

It has helped to make governments – the "distribution agencies of welfare" – into the exceedingly powerful institutions that they are today.

Mill's Utilitarian Reply

John Stuart Mill (1806–73) was rigorously crammed with education by his authoritarian father. He had a nervous breakdown at the age of 20, but recovered, partly as a result of his affair with a married woman – Mrs Harriet Taylor. His most famous works are *On Liberty* (1859), *The Subjection of Women* (1869) and *Utilitarianism* (1863). Mill redefined Bentham's philosophy in several ways.

UTILITARIANISM SHOULD TAKE SOME ACCOUNT OF "CONSCIENCE", EVEN THOUGH IT IS WHOLLY SUBJECTIVE, INACCESSIBLE TO PUBLIC SCRUTINY AND UNMEASURABLE.

THE WEALTH OF PROSPEROUS ENTREPRENEURS SHOULD BE TAXED TO A LIMITED DEGREE THAT WILL NOT DISCOURAGE THEIR INCENTIVE TO PRODUCE MORE.

IT IS INADVISABLE FOR ANYONE TO BREAK TRADITIONAL MORAL RULES, EVEN IF IT WOULD BENEFIT GREATER NUMBERS OF PEOPLE.

So Mill is sometimes thought of as a "Rule Utilitarian" – you obey those rules that experience has shown tend to produce large amounts of happiness, rather than judge each individual act on its utilitarian merits.

Qualifying the Majority

Mill's main concern was that Utilitarianism seemed to sanction the tyranny of the majority, so he tried to introduce *quality* as well as quantity into "felicific calculations". Bentham had famously insisted that "pushpin is equal to poetry" – if what the majority wants is a trivial pub game, then that is what they should get, regardless of its perceived merits.

A view which makes Utilitarianism less democratic and mildly élitist.

Representation by the Educated

Mill's paternalistic tendencies also emerged in his defence of representative democracy. It is wise to vote for highly educated middle-class professionals because they will act as a restraining influence on public opinion which is often uninformed and easy to manipulate.

SO QUITE HOW MEMBERS OF PARLIAMENT "REPRESENT" THEIR ELECTORATE IS NOT CLEAR.

THE BEST GOVERNMENT MUST BE THE GOVERNMENT OF THE WISEST, AND THESE MUST ALWAYS BE A FEW.

In *On Liberty*, Mill advocated that individual eccentricities and personal preferences should be tolerated by the majority, provided no one was harmed. The law should have little to say about personal lifestyles or sexual preferences.

In Defence of Democracy

Mill was one of the great defenders of the democratic "Ship of State". Citizens able to determine and change government policies are more likely to consent to being governed. Plato's benign dictatorship of experts treats people like irresponsible children, not citizens.

> LET A PERSON HAVE NOTHING TO DO FOR HIS COUNTRY AND HE WILL NOT CARE FOR IT.

> ACTIVE PARTICIPATION IN POLITICS HAS A DIRECT EDUCATIVE VALUE FOR THE ELECTORATE.

> FREEDOM OF SPEECH ENABLES "RECEIVED TRUTHS" TO BE CONTINUALLY CHALLENGED IN A PERMANENT STRUGGLE BETWEEN POLITICAL IDEAS.

POLITICAL TRUTHS, IF THEY EXIST AT ALL, SHOULD ALWAYS BE OPENLY CHALLENGED, SO THAT THE TRUEST SURVIVE.

Mill famously exercised his own freedom of speech, notably in his argument for complete economic and political equality for women – a view that, ironically, Plato had championed over 2,000 years before.

Modern Utilitarianism

Not many modern Utilitarians now believe that morality or politics can be made "scientific". There are no moral "facts" and it is probably not even desirable that there should be. And there is no convincing way of "proving" Utilitarianism.

> EVEN IF IT WERE POSSIBLE TO PROVE THAT INDIVIDUALS ALWAYS DESIRE THEIR OWN HAPPINESS, WHY DOES THAT OBLIGE THEM TO PROMOTE THE HAPPINESS OF OTHERS?

Modern Utilitarians prefer to talk about maximizing people's "interests" or "preferences", in order to avoid all of the practical and theoretical problems that occur with terms like "pleasure" and "happiness".

Rights and Minority Interests

Some political philosophers still believe in the importance of individual human rights. They can be used as a "trump card" by a minority to challenge any persecution sanctioned by the "interests" of a tyrannical majority.

Distribution and Equality

Utilitarianism's doctrine of maximizing happiness inevitably raises the problematic issue of economic equality. People are not born equal – some are more intelligent or gifted at certain things than others – and governments can't do much about that.

THEY CAN, HOWEVER, MAKE PEOPLE POLITICALLY EQUAL BY GIVING EVERYONE THE VOTE, THE RIGHT TO TRIAL BY JURY, AND SO ON.

BUT CAN OR SHOULD GOVERNMENTS ATTEMPT TO MAKE EVERYONE ECONOMICALLY EQUAL? SHOULD INDIVIDUALS WHO ARE FINANCIALLY WELL OFF BE COERCED INTO SUBSIDIZING POORER MEMBERS OF SOCIETY?

WON'T THAT GIVE THE STATE THE POWER TO INTERFERE WITH INDIVIDUAL LIBERTIES IN AN UNACCEPTABLE WAY?

Nozick's Political Philosophy

This problem of distribution has dominated much American political philosophy ever since **Robert Nozick** (1938–2002) published his book *Anarchy, State and Utopia* in 1974. He argued that it is not the state's job to impose its own "pattern" or "end state" onto its citizens. To bring about economic equality would mean the state interfering unacceptably with individual liberties. A great deal depends on how concepts like "justice" and "property" get defined.

IF, LIKE MARX AND MANY ANARCHIST PHILOSOPHERS, YOU BELIEVE THAT PROPERTY IS "CONGEALED LABOUR", THEN IT IS A FORM OF "THEFT" AND SHOULD BE REDISTRIBUTED.

BUT MOST PROPERTY HAS BEEN ACQUIRED QUITE FAIRLY. IT HASN'T BEEN STOLEN BY ITS OWNERS.

SO WE POSSESS THE FUNDAMENTAL LOCKEAN FREEDOM TO RETAIN IT AND DO WHAT WE WANT WITH IT.

Wealth belongs to individuals, in Nozick's view; it isn't "collective". If the state taxes earnings in order to redistribute them, then it is really engaging in a kind of "forced labour", because individuals are compelled to spend some of their time working to pay the government.

Equality of Opportunity

The usual liberal way of reaching a compromise on the problem of economic equality is to talk instead about "equality of opportunity", rather than insisting on any redistribution of actual wealth and earnings.

Individual liberties are not interfered with, and market forces are left alone to create and distribute wealth according to merit – and luck!

THE LIBERAL CONSENSUS IS THAT UNIVERSAL EDUCATION, HEALTHCARE AND EVEN SOCIAL HOUSING SHOULD BE WHOLLY OR PARTLY FUNDED BY THE STATE.

BUT THE LIBERTARIAN NOZICK OBJECTS EVEN TO THESE KINDS OF SOCIAL COMMITMENT ...

THEY CAN ONLY BE FUNDED THROUGH TAXATION, AND THAT LEADS TO MORE INTERFERENCE WITH INDIVIDUAL LIBERTIES.

REDISTRIBUTION OF WEALTH

SOCIAL WELFARE

The Minimal State

In Nozick's view, the fundamental rights of property are absolute and override any communal wellbeing. This means that the role of the state should be "minimal" – restricted almost exclusively to foreign policy. Even police protection should be privatized.

SO, FOR ME, THE DISTRIBUTION PROBLEM IS REALLY ABOUT PLACING STRICT LIMITS TO STATE POWER.

BOTH ARISTOTLE AND I THOUGHT THAT DISPROPORTIONATE WEALTH GAVE A FEW INDIVIDUALS DISPROPORTIONATE POLITICAL POWER.

IN MY BOOK **UTILITARIANISM**, I INSISTED THAT A DESIRE FOR PERSONAL HAPPINESS SOMEHOW ENTAILS THE HAPPINESS OF ALL ...

But if total freedom from government interference produces a society containing large numbers of ignorant, unemployed and homeless citizens, then most people would think that the moral and political costs of absolute personal liberty were too excessive. Providing everyone with a minimum standard of living would be more humane, and might even invalidate Marx's predictions about the inevitability of revolution. Economic justice could be good for the rich as well as the poor.

Rawls' Thought Experiment

Nozick's book was partly a right-wing Libertarian reply to *A Theory of Justice* (1971) by **John Rawls** (b. 1921), which drastically changed the agenda of contemporary political philosophy. Rawls reintroduced "contractualism" as a useful conceptual device, not to justify political authority but to argue for a limited form of economic justice.

The German philosopher **Immanuel Kant** (1724–1804) thought that universally agreed contracts could be a kind of "moral compass" …

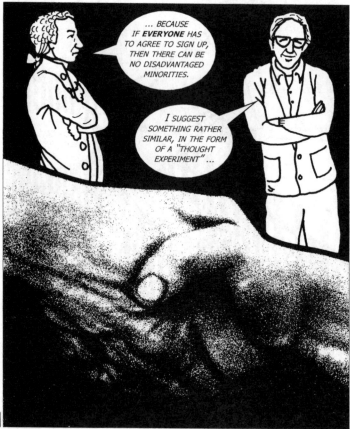

… BECAUSE IF **EVERYONE** HAS TO AGREE TO SIGN UP, THEN THERE CAN BE NO DISADVANTAGED MINORITIES.

I SUGGEST SOMETHING RATHER SIMILAR, IN THE FORM OF A "THOUGHT EXPERIMENT" …

You have to imagine that you are in a hypothetical "original position" (rather similar to a "state of nature").

You are also subjected to "a veil of ignorance", so that you know nothing about your place in society, gender, religious views, moral beliefs, political or philosophical ideologies.

This ostensibly converts you, and everybody else, into rational and moral individuals with fairly average attitudes towards risk, social justice and benevolence.

I THEN ASK YOU TO INVENT A SOCIETY THAT WOULD SUIT YOUR NEEDS AND DESIRES.

Rawlsian Society

Rawls maintains that nearly everyone would want to live in a society in which individual liberties were respected and where justice was universal and public.

Rawls concludes that all rational individuals would prefer societies that engage in some form of wealth redistribution. This fact should be considered by real governments when they frame domestic policy. But if each rational individual decides on the basis that he or she could be "any person", then it's difficult to see how this is a "contract" with anybody else.

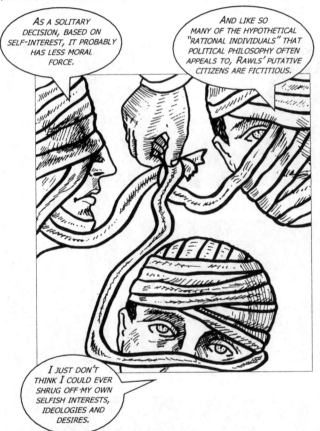

AS A SOLITARY DECISION, BASED ON SELF-INTEREST, IT PROBABLY HAS LESS MORAL FORCE.

AND LIKE SO MANY OF THE HYPOTHETICAL "RATIONAL INDIVIDUALS" THAT POLITICAL PHILOSOPHY OFTEN APPEALS TO, RAWLS' PUTATIVE CITIZENS ARE FICTITIOUS.

I JUST DON'T THINK I COULD EVER SHRUG OFF MY OWN SELFISH INTERESTS, IDEOLOGIES AND DESIRES.

Nozick's right-wing libertarians would probably still vote for a society that rewarded individual effort and self-sufficiency. They would be prepared to accept the risk of poverty, in exchange for high rewards and no state interference. Does this choice somehow make them "irrational"?

Totalitarian States

Countless 20th-century citizens have had to survive especially unpleasant totalitarian political regimes, both Fascist and Communist. Some political philosophers maintain that the roots of all such "closed societies" are already present in the philosophies of Plato, Hegel and Marx. But actual modern "Communist" states bore little relation to the theoretical ideals of Marx.

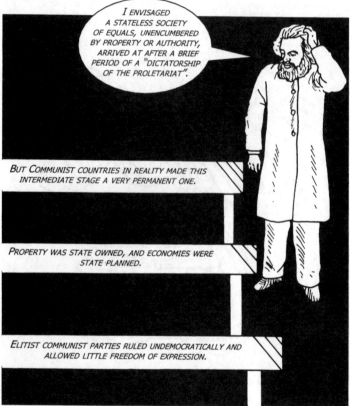

I ENVISAGED A STATELESS SOCIETY OF EQUALS, UNENCUMBERED BY PROPERTY OR AUTHORITY, ARRIVED AT AFTER A BRIEF PERIOD OF A "DICTATORSHIP OF THE PROLETARIAT".

BUT COMMUNIST COUNTRIES IN REALITY MADE THIS INTERMEDIATE STAGE A VERY PERMANENT ONE.

PROPERTY WAS STATE OWNED, AND ECONOMIES WERE STATE-PLANNED.

ELITIST COMMUNIST PARTIES RULED UNDEMOCRATICALLY AND ALLOWED LITTLE FREEDOM OF EXPRESSION.

In spite of their often genuine commitment to economic equality and social welfare, when the Communist regimes of the USSR and Eastern Europe collapsed, their citizens celebrated.

So where do totalitarian states come from and how can they be avoided in future? Social, as well as "psychological", explanations have been proposed by philosophers.

FASCISM WAS EMBRACED BY WORRIED "INAUTHENTIC" INDIVIDUALS SEARCHING FOR A COMFORTING GROUP IDENTITY.

MANY INDIVIDUALS POSSESS "AUTHORITARIAN PERSONALITIES" WHICH MAKE THEM EXPERIENCE AGGRESSIVE FEELINGS TOWARDS MINORITIES.

AUTHORITARIAN ATTITUDES ARE A "FLIGHT" FROM AN EXCESSIVE PERSONAL FREEDOM THAT MANY MODERN INDIVIDUALS FIND THREATENING.

PEOPLE LIKE TO BE TOLD WHAT TO THINK.

PSYCHOANALYST ERICH FROMM (1900–80).

JEAN-PAUL SARTRE (1905–80). MARXIST T.W. ADORNO (1903–69). PSYCHOANALYST WILHELM REICH (1897–1957).

Are Philosophers to Blame?

The philosopher of science **Karl Popper** (1902–94) argued that the seeds of repressive societies were sown by political philosophers themselves – Plato, Rousseau, Hegel and Marx. Totalitarian societies tend to be teleological and utopian. Utopianists tend to be dogmatic about ends and casual about means, with an unhealthy respect for uniformity and a dislike of human variety.

ADVOCATES OF "BLUEPRINT" SOCIETIES HAVE NO IDEA HOW THEIR VISIONARY IDEAS WILL WORK IN PRACTICE, AND ARE USUALLY RUTHLESS AGAINST THOSE WHO OPPOSE THEM.

YOU CANNOT BLAME US FOR THE CRIMINAL ABUSE OF OUR IDEAS …

We've already seen how those who oppose the perfect one-party rule of Plato's "Guardians" or Rousseau's "General Will" are not to be tolerated. And there are undoubtedly strains of absolutism and élitism in their political philosophies. Nevertheless, they might justifiably protest about retrospective interpretations made of their work.

Is Pluralist Society Best?

Totalitarian states rely on a pessimistic view of human nature. Human beings are irrational, irresponsible and need determined leaders aware of citizens' real needs, regardless of expressed preferences. Liberals instead believe that there can be no ideal political society and therefore no **absolute** political ideologies.

THE HEALTHIEST SOCIETIES ARE PLURALIST AND TOLERATE A WIDE RANGE OF DIFFERING POLITICAL OPINIONS.

MOST MODERN WESTERNERS WOULD AGREE WITH THAT.

BUT RADICAL PHILOSOPHERS LIKE HERBERT MARCUSE WOULD STILL ARGUE THAT OUR OWN CAPITALIST SOCIETIES DISPLAY TOTALITARIAN FEATURES.

OUR SOCIETIES CAN BE EXTREMELY INTOLERANT OF VIEWS OUTSIDE THE LIBERAL CONSENSUS.

GLOBAL CORPORATIONS CAN SEEM AS REPRESSIVE AS ANY TOTALITARIAN GOVERNMENT.

The Limits on Freedom

What is "political freedom" that we value it so highly? Most political philosophers assume that we possess free will, whilst also admitting that we are conditioned to accept limited kinds of political choice. Most citizens accept that absolute personal freedom is an illusion – we have to accept some kind of "collective freedom" to function as members of groups and as responsible citizens. The liberal thinker **Isaiah Berlin** (1909–97) famously suggested that political freedom can be both "negative" and "positive".

> *NEGATIVE FREEDOM MEANS THAT WE HAVE CERTAIN "RIGHTS" THAT PLACE LIMITS ON HOW FAR THE STATE CAN INTERFERE IN OUR LIVES.*

> *POSITIVE FREEDOM MEANS THAT WE ARE ENTITLED TO CERTAIN OPPORTUNITIES AND CHOICES WITH WHICH TO DEVELOP OUR POTENTIAL AS HUMAN BEINGS.*

Right-wing democratic governments tend to favour the idea of negative liberty because a state that interferes with individual freedom reduces the individual's self-reliance and initiative. Left-wing governments counter this with the belief that no one can be truly "free" who is denied the opportunity to succeed because of poverty and a lack of education.

Berlin argues that the provision of positive liberty almost inevitably harms certain kinds of "negative" liberty.

> WE ALWAYS INSISTED THAT "FREEDOM" MEANS "OBEDIENCE" BECAUSE THE STATE IS THE EXTERNAL MANIFESTATION OF THE WILL OF EVERY INDIVIDUAL.

ROUSSEAU   HEGEL   MARCUSE

> THAT'S WHY I SAY THAT "NEGATIVE" FREEDOM MUST ALWAYS TAKE PRECEDENCE ...

> GOVERNMENTS CAN ALL TOO EASILY DISGUISE THE LOSS OF NEGATIVE FREEDOM WITH PROMISES OF THE MORE POSITIVE KIND.

> YOU OVERLOOK THAT MOST PEOPLE SUFFER FROM "FALSE CONSCIOUSNESS" AND ARE MUCH LESS FREE THAN THEY REALIZE.

Marcuse, a postmodern Marxist, furthered the idea that we are the happy slaves of capitalism, denied any real freedom to protest because our "uni-dimensional" democracy is designed to foreclose on all new forms of radical thought.

Why Should We Obey?

Utilitarians like Bentham and Mill justify our obedience to the state simply because it is to our advantage. The state provides us with security, allows for the impartial application of law which, in turn, gives us freedom. The existence of states also indirectly encourages wealth-creation, which can then be used for public welfare. Rousseau and Hegel held that it is false to think of citizens and the State as separate entities.

However, in spite of what they all may say, political philosophers can never conclusively "prove" that they are right.

Communitarian Aristotelians

Liberals agree it is not the state's job to impose its own "teleological" views onto millions of individual strangers all chasing their own varieties of personal fulfilment. But, recently, "virtue" philosophers like the "Aristotelian" **Alasdair MacIntyre** (b. 1929) have questioned this core wisdom of liberal ideology.

HUMAN BEINGS AREN'T JUST SOCIALLY DISCONNECTED AND DISEMBODIED INDIVIDUALS WITH "RIGHTS". THEY ALSO NEED A WELL-FUNCTIONING COMMUNITY IN ORDER TO "FLOURISH".

HUMAN BEINGS RELATE TO EACH OTHER IN COMMUNAL WAYS THAT AREN'T EXCLUSIVELY ECONOMIC.

INDIVIDUAL ECONOMIC FREEDOM MAY BE IMPORTANT BUT IS NOT THE ONLY MORAL AND POLITICAL VALUE …

ESPECIALLY WHEN IT HAS THE UNDESIRABLE SIDE-EFFECTS OF IMPOVERISHMENT AND POLITICAL DISORDER.

But modern pluralist societies have no universal traditions, customs or religious beliefs any more, which makes it very difficult to determine exactly what "community life" actually entails.

Liberals would say it is not the job of a paternalist state to foster "community life" because this would considerably extend its power – and extensive state power is always abused.

Postmodernist Politics

The crucial postmodernist political text remains *The Postmodern Condition* (1979) by **Jean-François Lyotard** (b. 1924). It announced the collapse of "Grand Narratives" like that of the Enlightenment, which naively believed in the possibility of absolute political progress, and Marxism, which failed to impose its theoretical and determinist pattern on unpredictable human beings. Postmodernists delight in exposing Western political philosophy's reliance on "totalizing" theories which impose "order" and endorse the state's monopoly of "legitimate" force. Postmodernists deconstruct the "absolute truths" of political philosophy to reveal how they are always relative.

Lyotard ends his essay by recommending a more diverse series of "small political narratives", but is splendidly vague about what kinds of institutions might be required to arbitrate between different "narratives".

Knowledge and Power

Michel Foucault (1926–84) was another postmodernist philosopher who challenged the idea of history as a narrative of continuing rationality and progress. He stressed that knowledge and power are always related. Each society has its "general politics" of truth: the types of discourse which it accepts and enforces as acceptable knowledge.

THE MODERN STATE RARELY HAS TO RESORT TO ANY OVERT DISPLAY OF FORCE BECAUSE ITS CITIZENS ARE ALREADY HIGHLY DISCIPLINED "SUBJECTS" WITH AN INNER LIFE THAT IS ONLY MARGINALLY THEIR OWN.

POLITICAL PHILOSOPHIES FOUNDED ON WHATEVER THEORY OF HUMAN NATURE ARE IDEOLOGICAL FALSEHOODS BECAUSE THERE IS NO ONE "TRUE" HUMAN PARADIGM.

NOTHING IN MAN, NOT EVEN HIS BODY, IS SUFFICIENTLY STABLE TO SERVE AS THE BASIS FOR SELF-RECOGNITION OR FOR UNDERSTANDING OTHER MEN.

The state is a mythical abstraction whose importance is a lot more limited than many of us think. This is because power – and all struggles to obtain it or escape from it – is an inescapable feature of all social relations. The state is merely one rather abstract reflection of this fact.

Environmental Politics

Political philosophy isn't just about the state's right to exist. Environmental politics is now of major interest to most of us. People want to conserve the Earth's resources, protect their local environment, use appropriate technologies and value what wildernesses remain. The political and economic ideology of classical liberalism with its defence of self-interest is undoubtedly much to blame for the depletion of the world's resources and a reduction in the quality of life for many citizens in the West.

Modern democratic governments constantly have to make "cost-benefit" decisions on what levels of pollution are "acceptable". They can use different forms of punitive taxation to ensure that some economic activities become no longer profitable.

BUT THE MOST SERIOUS ENVIRONMENTAL PROBLEMS — LIKE GLOBAL WARMING AND THE DEPLETION OF THE OZONE LAYER — CAN ONLY BE TACKLED BY AGREEMENTS BETWEEN NATIONS.

BUT ALL OF THEM HAVE DIFFERENT INTERESTS TO DEFEND AND AGENDAS TO PURSUE.

CAPITALIST ECONOMICS CLEARLY NEEDS TO CHANGE TO SUSTAINABILITY AND ENVIRONMENTAL STABILITY.

AND POLITICIANS HAVE TO REFLECT ON HOW THIS CAN BE ACHIEVED.

A new kind of "holistic" political philosophy needs to be invented which is more communitarian and aware of the fact that we "political animals" are only a part of this planet and not its master.

Feminist Politics

The feminist movement is itself a direct offshoot of the Enlightenment political ideal of equality. **Mary Wollstonecraft** (1759–97) was the first among many feminists to argue the case for equality.

But many feminists now maintain that "equality" is always defined by "universal" norms which remain essentially masculine.

Athenian male citizens could only participate in their democratic lives because of disenfranchized armies of women and slaves. Even recent political philosophers like John Rawls still cling to the odd idea that ideal rational observers can somehow discard their gender as "clothing".

Consumers and Citizens

Our postmodern capitalist societies are still dominated by a liberal ideology which believes that freedom is best guaranteed by free-market global capitalism and minimal state interference. Most of us Westerners have now internalized capitalism, so that we have come to think of ourselves more as consumers than citizens.

CAPITALISM ENSURES THAT IT IS NOT THE PEOPLE THAT ARE IN CHARGE BUT THEIR MANUFACTURED DESIRES.

BUT EVEN THIS "GRAND NARRATIVE" CANNOT CONTINUE FOR EVER ...

CAPITALIST GROWTH WILL EVENTUALLY BE CHECKED BY THE PLANET'S FINITE RESOURCES, IF NOT BY A WORKERS' REVOLUTION.

JÜRGEN HABERMAS

*THE RELUCTANT POSTMODERNIST **JÜRGEN HABERMAS** (B. 1929) FORESEES THAT WESTERN GOVERNMENTS WILL INCREASINGLY CONFRONT A "LEGITIMATION CRISIS".*

*GOVERNMENTS CANNOT SATISFY THE DEMANDS OF GLOBAL CAPITALISM **AND** THEN AVOID THE SOCIAL CRISES THAT CAPITALISM ITSELF CAUSES.*

Healthy democratic societies are cemented together by a moral consensus based on pre-capitalist values of trust and mutual support, whereas capitalism is motivated by self-interest and competition. It is difficult to see how this circle can ever be convincingly squared.

Democracy by Choice

In the end, all theories are attempts to describe and explain reality, but political theories are unlike scientific theories in that they are impossible to verify conclusively. This is because, ultimately, they are theories about who we are or how we should live together. That's why there are so many different kinds of political philosophy. Some philosophers believe in the possibility of objective rational answers to political problems based on a knowledge of fundamental human needs, goals, purposes and relationships. Others insist that this sort of knowledge is impossible in the face of wholly unpredictable individual preferences and desires. Much political philosophy may, in the end, turn out to be inescapably subjective – merely well-argued expressions of personal preferences. But that doesn't mean that some theories cannot be more productive than others by helping to change how we see ourselves and our political societies. But we probably **do** have to accept that the modern state, with all of its surveillance and military technology, is now virtually unchallengeable and "democratic" only in a very limited sense. "Politics" will have to change profoundly if citizens are to regain any real power. Mature adult individuals might eventually decide to ignore huge and impersonal modern nation states and decide instead to meet face-to-face in small assemblies to discuss those policies and practices that determine their everyday lives.

Further Reading

All the books mentioned in this one are readily available in paperback. Most of them are very readable, although no one has ever described Hegel as "accessible".

Theodor Adorno et al., *The Authoritarian Personality* (Harper and Bros., 1950)

St Aquinas, *Selected Political Writings* (Blackwell, 1959)

Aristotle, *Nichomachean Ethics* (Oxford University Press, 1975) and *The Politics* (Clarendon Press, 1958)

St Augustine, *City of God* (Penguin, 1972)

S. Bentham and J.S. Mill, *Utilitarianism and Other Essays* (Penguin, 1987)

Edmund Burke, *Reflections on the Revolution in France* (Penguin, 1969)

Francis Fukuyama, *The End of History and the Last Man* (Penguin, 1993)

Antonio Gramsci, *Gramsci's Writings on the State and Hegemony 1916–35* (University of Birmingham Press, 1997)

G.W.F. Hegel, *The Philosophy of Right* (Great Books in Philosophy, 1996)

Thomas Hobbes, *Leviathan* (Penguin, 1981)

John Locke, *Two Treatises of Government* (Cambridge University Press, 1967)

Jean-François Lyotard, *The Postmodern Condition* (Manchester University Press, 1984)

Niccolo Machiavelli, *The Prince* (Cambridge University Press, 1988)

Herbert Marcuse, *One-Dimensional Man* (Routledge, 1991)

Karl Marx, *Capital* (Abridged) (Oxford World Classics, 1988); Marx and Friedrich Engels, *The German Ideology* (Great Books in Philosophy, 1998) and *The Communist Manifesto* (Penguin, 1967)

John Stuart Mill, *On Liberty* (Penguin, 1985)

Robert Nozick, *Anarchy, State and Utopia* (Blackwell, 1974)

Thomas Paine, *The Rights of Man* (Penguin, 1976)

Plato, *The Republic*, trans. M.D.P. Lee (Penguin, 1972)

John Rawls, *A Theory of Justice* (Oxford University Press, 1973)

Jean Jacques Rousseau, *The Social Contract* (Penguin, 1970)

Mary Wollstonecraft, *A Vindication of the Rights of Women* (Penguin, 1992)

The *Introducing* series also has guides to Plato, Aristotle, Rousseau, Hegel, Marx and Foucault, and other titles on philosophy that are helpful.

Two short and readable general books about political philosophy are Brian Redhead, *From Plato to Nato* (BBC Books, 1988), and Jonathan Wolff, *An Introduction to Political Philosophy* (Oxford University Press, 2001).

Man and Society by John Plamenatz (Longman, 1963) is a rather more scholarly introduction to all modern political philosophers from Machiavelli to Marx. Plamenatz describes and analyzes their work with considerable

clarity. Barbara Goodwin's *Using Political Ideas* (John Wiley and Sons, 1982) is a very useful guide to all of the major political ideologies.

A History of Political Thought by John Morrow (New York University Press, 1998) takes an interesting approach to the subject. And two other books useful for those who wish to find out more are Andrew Vincent, *Theories of the State* (Blackwell, 1987), and Raymond Plant, *Modern Political Thought* (Blackwell, 1991).

The Blackwell Encyclopaedia of Political Thought (1991) provides overall views of topics like "Obligation" and "Consent" as well as brief guides to all the major writers. Other useful reference works are *The Penguin Dictionary of Politics* (1993) and *A Dictionary of Political Thought* (Macmillan, 1983).

A Companion to Contemporary Political Philosophy (Blackwell, 1995) contains essays by many contemporary political philosophers on a wide range of subjects. *The Politics of Postmodernity* (Cambridge University Press, 1998) is another recent collection of essays that is well worth reading.

Karl Popper argues against the system-builders Plato, Rousseau, Hegel and Marx in *The Open Society and Its Enemies* (Routledge, 1969). *Journey Through Utopia* by Marie Louise Berneri (Freedom Press, 1982) reveals the authoritarian aspect of utopianists. *Demanding the Impossible: A History of Anarchism* by Peter Marshall (HarperCollins, 1993) offers salutory criticism of arguments supporting the State.

About the author and artist

Dave Robinson has taught philosophy to students for many years. He is the author of several other Icon books, including those on Plato and Rousseau. His more radical friends believe him to be a harmless "armchair anarchist".

Judy Groves has illustrated many of the Icon "Introducing" series, including *Wittgenstein*, *Philosophy*, *Plato*, *Aristotle* and *Bertrand Russell*.

Acknowledgements

The author would like to thank his indefatigable editor, Richard Appignanesi, who always knows how to convert disorganized manuscripts into readable books. He is also grateful for the illustrations and subtle alterations of emphasis provided by his artistic colleague. He would also like to thank all of his friends for being endlessly impatient with his own half-baked political opinions, which are, of course, always infallibly correct.

The artist would like to thank Oscar Zarate for the illustrations on pages 20, 27, 30, 87, 92, 140 and 150. She also thanks David King for the loan of photographs from his collection.

Index